A MEASURE OF MY HEART

LIFE LESSONS FROM YOGI

PAUL LESSARD

A MEASURE OF MY HEART

LIFE LESSONS FROM YOGI

"Life shrinks or expands in proportion to one's courage."

~ Anais Nin

ALSO BY PAUL LESSARD:

The Mean Little Princess

Visions of Philanthropy

For information regarding special discounts for bulk purchases,
Please contact AMeasureofMyHeart.com

Designed by The McNeill Communications Group Inc.

Printed in the United States of America

Library of Congress Cataloging in Publication Data
Paul Lessard, 2013

A MEASURE OF MY HEART
~ Life Lessons From Yogi ~

ISBN 978-0-9897295-0-5

This book is for my friend, Yogi, who taught me to lead with my heart, love with passion and always to remember that God is still good even in the darkest of times.

To my dear friend Martha, Yogi's beloved wife, who is a woman of courage, faith and beauty — thank you for allowing me to take this journey with Yogi.

To Yogi's sons, Preston and Scott — you are blessed to have shared a very special love with your father who considered you both his soul mates and treasures.

FOREWORD

A MESSAGE FROM MDA ON ITS
URGENT MISSION TO MAKE LIFE BETTER
FOR FAMILIES FIGHTING ALS

Amyotrophic lateral sclerosis (ALS) is a challenging disease, and those facing it need to know that they are never alone. MDA, the Muscular Dystrophy Association, is here to help. MDA is the only nonprofit health agency in the world dedicated to fighting ALS and more than 40 other neuromuscular diseases with comprehensive research, health care services, advocacy and education programs.

At MDA, we've understood for decades that when an individual is affected by ALS, the entire family needs help and support, too. Some of our leading ALS clinicians have referred to ALS as "nice guy's disease" because so many of the men and women affected are marked by unusual qualities of decency and compassion. Other observers have noted that many with ALS are high achievers, having made significant contributions in sports, politics, business, the arts and sciences and other fields. People with ALS are moms and dads, sons and daughters, all with their own hopes, abilities and dreams. They are our friends, neighbors and loved ones.

Since inception, MDA has dedicated almost $325 million to ALS research and health care services. Our status as a world leader in the fight against ALS has its beginnings way back in the 1950s. That's when Eleanor Gehrig, widow of baseball legend Lou Gehrig, joined with MDA as a result of her search for a meaningful way of striking back against the disease that took her husband's life. She served for more than a decade as MDA's National Campaign Chairperson, and her passion has continued to energize and guide us in our ongoing effort to discover treatments and cures to help those with ALS.

MDA has funded more ALS research than any other voluntary health organization in the United States. In 2014, we supported 64 ALS grants with a total commitment of over $17 million. MDA supports early-stage research into what causes ALS, as well as studies of potential therapeutic targets, with the hope that clinical trials will ensue leading to treatments. It's part of our research investment philosophy to nurture game-changing thinking by encouraging young investigators to commit to studying ALS and related neuromuscular diseases.

In 2014, those with ALS and their families received help from top health professionals skilled in the diagnosis and medical management of ALS through MDA's nationwide network of nearly 190 specialized neuromuscular disease clinics, including more than 40 designated ALS centers.

We provide practical support as well, such as help in locating and repairing durable medical equipment, while also assisting individuals and caregivers to connect with other members of the ALS community through support groups and online social networks. In addition, MDA helps families mobilize a personal support network through myMuscleteam, a care coordination tool. ALS families stay informed with the help of research updates and in-depth articles provided through our website and publications.

Here are some other facts about MDA services to help those with ALS:

- MDA operates an ALS Clinical Research Network, housed at five of the largest ALS research centers in the country. MDA pioneered the use of historical controls in ALS clinical trial design, reducing the number of patients needed for trials and increasing the efficiency of clinical testing for new therapies.

- MDA hosts international conferences every year attended by hundreds of leading scientists, clinicians and drug developers, to inspire collaboration and innovation in the quest to design, discover and deliver new therapies as rapidly as possible.

- Through MDA's advocacy efforts and community events, we actively influence public policy, and have joined with other leaders in the ALS community to testify before the FDA to address the unique needs of ALS patients and their families.

- MDA's Neuromuscular Disease Registry is helping optimize clinical outcomes and evaluate best practices in ALS care.

- Our "umbrella organization" status puts us in a unique position to leverage the advances in research and best practices for clinical care from one disease to inform progress in others.

At MDA, we're committed to continuing to provide comprehensive care to ALS families while accelerating research progress that will lead to the definitive medical answers so many are waiting for. Together, we will defeat ALS.

For more information, or to donate or volunteer to support progress in MDA's fight against ALS, please visit **mda.org**. Thank you.

ACKNOWLEDGEMENTS

This book chronicles a very personal journey with a man I loved and admired from the first day we met. I thank Yogi for trusting me with his legacy and for allowing me to walk with him through the final leg of his life's journey. It is a privilege to lock arms with a man of faith and courage, and to be welcomed into his heart where there are no places to hide.

A special thanks to my wife Jayne and my children, Taylor and Jordan, for putting up with the late nights and lost weekends that writing this book has entailed. Jayne, you are my hero, my best friend, my partner, my therapist and my daily inspiration. Thanks for loving me.

A MEASURE OF MY HEART

LIFE LESSONS FROM YOGI

CONTENTS

ALS... LEARNING ABOUT THE ENEMY

I come from a military family and was raised on books about warfare, tactics and strategy. I learned early that one must completely understand an opponent to effectively combat and ultimately defeat him. ALS is without doubt one of the most formidable opponents I have ever encountered, and since my friend Yogi died, I have made it my mission to help find a cure. I hope all of you who read this book will not only appreciate the life of a truly courageous man, but also join me in the fight to find a cure for ALS, a cure that is long overdue.

Here are a few facts about the enemy, which will help you appreciate the courage and determination of my friend Yogi and the thousands of other brave souls who have battled this disease:

ALS, or amyotrophic lateral sclerosis, is a motor neuron disease. Amyotrophic comes from the Greek language: "A" means no, "myo" refers to muscle, and "trophic" means nourishment. Amyotrophic therefore means "no muscle nourishment." Lateral identifies the areas in a person's spinal cord where portions of the nerve cells that are affected are located. As the area degenerates, it leads to scarring sclerosis, or hardening in the region.

ALS, also known as Lou Gehrig's disease or Maladie de Charcot, after Jean Martin Charcot, the French doctor who first identified it, is a progressive, fatal syndrome caused by the degeneration of motor neurons, the nerve cells in the central nervous system that control voluntary muscle movement. The disorder causes muscle weakness and atrophy throughout the body as both the upper and lower motor neurons degenerate, ceasing to send messages to the muscles. No test can provide a definite diagnosis of ALS; instead, the diagnosis of ALS is primarily based on the symptoms and the signs the physician observes in the patient and a series of tests to rule out other diseases.

The onset of ALS may be so subtle that the symptoms are frequently overlooked. The earliest symptoms are obvious weakness and/or muscle atrophy. This is followed by twitching, cramping or stiffness of affected muscles; muscle weakness affecting an arm or a leg; and/or slurred and nasal speech.

Regardless of the part of the body first affected by the disease, it is typical for muscle weakness and atrophy to spread to other parts of the body as the disease progresses. Eventually, people with ALS will not be able to stand or walk. In the latter stages of the disease, the diaphragm and intercostal muscles (muscles between the ribs) weaken, and the patient no longer has the strength or the ability to breathe. Although ventilation support can ease problems with breathing and prolong survival, it does not derail the progression of ALS. Most patients die from respiratory failure usually within three to five years from the onset of the symptoms.

INTRODUCTION

Yogi Yarborough was dying. ALS had silently crept into his body and would within months steal away an amazing life that had been marked by both miraculous blessings and heart-wrenching tragedies. Throughout his 61 years, Yogi rose above the challenges life threw in his path with determination and faith, which ultimately made him stronger and more grateful. The blessings, and there were many, were appreciated in a way that only those who rose up from dire circumstances can grasp. These blessings were always freely shared with those he loved and those who most needed his help.

This book is the culmination of a 25-year friendship and a remarkable series of lunchtime discussions that took place every Friday throughout the final 16 months of Yogi's life. It is a remembrance of my bittersweet journey with a man whom I loved and respected, who befriended and mentored me through most of my adult life.

It was a life-changing privilege to walk alongside my friend and bear witness to the values and principles that guided him through his remarkable life and sustained him during his final journey home. His generosity and compassion endeared him to everyone he met, and the love that returned to him through those relationships fortified him more than anyone will ever know.

He once told me that he was constantly amazed at how an illness like ALS could so completely eliminate all of those unnecessary distractions in life — the pressures of work, the volatility of the stock market and the hundreds of meaningless preoccupations that had once seemed so important. He would often share, without resentment, how the disease that gradually took away his independence, mobility and pride caused his world to grow infinitely smaller and how this brought so many unexpected blessings into his life. It was a shame, he would often say, that it took having a fatal disease to really open his eyes and enable him to understand the true priorities in life.

In his final months, Yogi became acutely aware of the importance of passing along the hard-earned lessons God had so faithfully provided over the years. This wisdom, born of a lifetime of rising above seemingly insurmountable challenges, was increasingly clarified by the realization of his rapidly dwindling time. Not only were these truths revealed through his battle with ALS, they also sprang up from the memories of a childhood spent in poverty, in the stories of his determination as a young man who struggled mightily to overcome insecurities and failures, and later in the recollections of an enormously successful businessman who grappled with the demands of family, business and the ghosts of his past.

Every life has a defining moment, a time in which one's heart and soul are exposed for each of us to behold our true mettle. For some, this moment is a divine revelation; for others, it is a fleeting vapor that simply appears and just as suddenly fades away, forever missed. For those who are fortunate enough to embrace this glimpse of the enormity of God's love revealed in the promise of our potential as well as his provision for our future, life is never the same.

Yogi experienced his moment many years ago in the chaos of a crowded, noisy locker room located deep in the bowels of the East Carolina University field house. Even now, I can see those young, eager athletes milling around the small but spunky running back from the little town of Reeds, North Carolina, biding their time in the weigh-in line. They no doubt gave little thought to the words their coach shouted across the room as the shortest member of their team stepped on the scale, but Yogi did. In fact, he never forgot them. He pressed them carefully into his heart, and they came to define a remarkable life of challenge, achievement, compassion, loss and love that would leave an indelible mark upon me and so many others who would have the privilege of knowing this special man.

The words that turned Yogi's head that day still echoed in his heart some 40 years later: "Don't measure that Yarborough boy unless you can put a tape measure around his heart!" In that moment, Yogi knew a man whom he greatly respected had seen something special in him. Today, decades later, these words whisper to me as I consider the age-old question of how do we, as a people and, indeed, as a culture, truly measure the heart of a good man?

Do we examine and evaluate his worldly achievements? If so, Yogi would certainly qualify. He was the 11th of 12 children, a talented athlete, first in his family to attend and graduate from college, a cancer survivor, a tremendously successful entrepreneur, a committed community leader, and a generous philanthropist.

Yet to know Yogi was to understand that while all these achievements are notable, the greatest accomplishments in his life were those driven by his heart. They include a longstanding love relationship with his God, a loving wife, devoted sons, beautiful grandchildren, loyal friends and the love of countless people whose lives he touched.

May this story be the "measure" that truly illustrates the depth and breadth of Yogi's brave and compassionate heart; one that each of us can share and forever carry with us as a reminder that life's most cherished gifts are faith, hope and love, but the greatest of these is love.

CHAPTER 1

THE VALUE OF THE STRUGGLE

HOW FALLING DOWN TEACHES US TO PULL OURSELVES UP

"The ultimate measure of a man is not where he stands
in moments of comfort and convenience, but where he stands
at times of challenge and controversy."

~ Dr. Martin Luther King, Jr., 1963

Yogi and I always shared a deep and abiding love affair with all that is barbecued, smoked or pit-roasted. To us and so many others in the South, barbecue is so much more than a culinary genre. It is actually considered by many, Yogi and me included, more akin to a cultural art form that is of true Southern origin.

So it wasn't unusual when a call arrived one morning from Yogi inviting me to join him for lunch that afternoon at the local barbecue establishment, a place known simply as "The Original" Lexington Barbecue. Needless to say, an invitation to share barbecue with a friend like Yogi at a place like The Original Lexington Barbecue is one that can never be taken lightly.

Yogi's call had caught me during an interesting juncture of my life. I was in my late 40s and had been married for almost 20 years to a wonderful woman. My home was replete with the angst, pathos and excitement that could only be wrought by two teenagers who brought equal parts light and terror into my life. My professional life was inspiring beyond my wildest dreams, yet there was a nagging feeling hovering constantly around me that seemed to insinuate that God still had something more in store for me.

Have you ever just sat back in your favorite chair, taken a deep breath and wished that somehow, some way, you could be a better person? That by some miraculous turn you could actually do and say and live in such a way that truly reflected your faith and your heart? That despite all the distractions of the world around you, there might be a way you could steal a brief glimpse of what God sees in your heart?

I had found myself pondering these questions with a disturbing degree of frequency over the weeks before Yogi's call. Little did I realize that his phone call would be my opportunity not only to observe the current state of my heart, but to delight in the rarest of all opportunities — to see God present himself in my life in a powerful and life-changing way.

On the afternoon of our lunch, Yogi seemed uncharacteristically subdued. He was walking with a cane, which reminded me of the recent back problems he had been experiencing that had hobbled his right leg.

As we worked our way through the meal, a special plate of pulled barbecue and slaw made by the cook just for Yogi, I watched how my friend playfully teased our waitress, inquired about her family and complimented her in his uniquely folksy way. Like most meals with Yogi, it was punctuated with introductions to friends, highlighted by stories of his family and concluded with our mutual scramble for the bill. Yogi won that day, and as he shuffled up to the register, I noticed our waitress watching Yogi as he moved haltingly toward the front of the restaurant. She looked on in silence, ever so slightly shaking her head, and it was only then that I realized she was crying.

After the meal, we cruised around the town of Lexington in Yogi's car. He showed me the school he attended as a boy and the houses to which he delivered newspapers. He took me to the spot where his family's home had been and carefully pointed out the houses that now belonged to his many brothers and sisters. We drove past the fields in which he had played ball as a young boy. The grass was green, the wind was blowing softly in the pines and I could almost see the kids playing ball. It was at this idyllic ball field that Yogi pulled his car slowly to the curb and turned off the engine.

I watched my friend take a deep breath, and I sensed that something was about to happen that would change everything. I suddenly wanted more time. I remembered that I had known this man for almost 25 years, and scenes from our friendship flashed through my mind. I first met him when his boys, Scott and Preston, attended a soccer camp at High Point College, the school where I played intercollegiate soccer and worked every summer teaching the game I had loved as long as I could remember. At this moment, sitting in Yogi's car in front of that ball field, I sensed that our relationship was about to take a very different course. My heart seemed to catch in the silence of anticipation.

Yogi's words were carefully measured and calm when he finally spoke. He was dying. He paused for an instant, then continued on with quiet conviction and absolute calm. Suddenly, there didn't seem to be enough air in the car, and I found myself struggling to comprehend the meaning of his words. They seemed to hang precariously in the air, resonating in that terrible moment, and I searched for something, anything, to say that might somehow refute his frightening news.

There had to be other alternatives, I thought. Hadn't we been hearing about these new experimental therapies that were miraculously saving lives? There had to be something that could fix this; that could take away this obscenely unfair prognosis from my friend who was such a good man, who was so beloved, so respected and who deserved to live a long and happy life. But when I looked up, I could see the finality in his expression. There was a sobering, heartbreaking acceptance in those dreaded words, yet there was no fear, just a keen sense of disappointment at the thought of events in the lives of those he loved that he would never see.

It was ALS, amyotrophic lateral sclerosis, an insidiously cruel disease that slowly robs its victims of their strength, their mobility, their independence and, ultimately, their lives. It is often referred to as Lou Gehrig's disease, the motor neuron illness that took one of baseball's most graceful players who had, despite his illness, once called himself the "Luckiest man on the face of the earth."

Yes, even then I knew enough about the illness to know that this was truly tragic news and that the prognosis was grim. I learned that a recent trip to the Mayo Clinic had confirmed the diagnosis that Yogi had received at Wake Forest Baptist Medical Center in Winston-Salem earlier that month.

Yogi gazed resolutely into my eyes as he told me that he was not afraid of dying, and I believed him. However, he was heartbroken over the thought of leaving the ones he loved, and he was absolutely devastated that he would never get to see his beloved grandchildren, Nathan and Maggie, grow up.

I was still numb. I felt stunned and breathless. As I caught myself tearing up, I heard my own voice, seemingly detached and distant, telling my friend how deeply sorry I was and how unfair it all was. It was only then that I realized that Yogi had reached across the console and was holding my hand. My dying friend was comforting me.

He looked at me with a curious combination of joy and grief. Then he actually smiled as he told me that he would never ask, "Why me?" In fact, he went one step further. He told me he would remind himself every day to ask, "Why not me?" He assured me that he had lived an especially blessed life, a life that had given him so much more then he had ever deserved. God had been more than good to him. Even then, in the midst of this horrific prognosis, Yogi reminded me that his God, our God, was still good.

His smile became brighter as he shared his heartfelt belief that God would enable something truly powerful to come out of his season of struggle, something that he hoped would touch the lives of others. Maybe, he surmised, it would be something so much bigger than his own life, and maybe – just maybe – he would have the courage and grace to see it through, and that with God's help he would finish with faith, dignity and grace.

I listened with both awe and wonder as my friend acknowledged God's provision and love even in the face of this bleak and frightening future. I was humbled by his strength and his amazing grace. I slowly began to realize that I was indeed in the presence of a man who, with the help of his God and his friends, could face down this terrible challenge and rise above it.

Yogi must have seen the light bulb in my head switch on, for he gave me a nod of acknowledgement, squeezed my hand a final time, inserted the key in the ignition and started the car. As we pulled away from the baseball field, he asked me, in a tone that seemed to undo all the confusion and pain, if I would do him the honor of delivering his eulogy when the time came.

Would I deliver his eulogy? Would I tell the story of his life and share his final thoughts and dreams to those he loved most? Of course, I would. I determined at that very moment I would tell his wife, his children, his grandchildren and all of his friends what I loved and admired most about this special man ... my friend, my mentor and now my guide, who so willingly embraced the monumental struggle that lay ahead.

Yogi knew then, as I know now, that facing disaster, falling down and struggling was not the terrible experience so many of us spend our lives trying to avoid. It is instead a gift that God lovingly uses to teach each of us about the true power of the faith, goodness and strength that so often lies untapped and dormant in our hearts. Yogi may have been dying that day, but in a lot of respects, he and, by extension, I had never been as intensely alive as we were together in that moment staring down death with the knowledge that God was indeed in control, even if we were not.

CHAPTER 2

THE JOY CONUNDRUM

UNDERSTANDING THAT JOY IS A SELF-INFLICTED
WOUND THAT ONLY OCCURS WHEN WE
CHOOSE TO LOOK BEYOND OURSELVES

*"The purpose of life is not to be happy. It is to be useful,
to be honorable, to be compassionate, to have it make some difference
that you have lived and lived well."*

~ Ralph Waldo Emerson

Autumn has always been my favorite time of the year. It brings back memories of soccer games, cross-country races, leisurely picnics with warm wool blankets, brisk New Hampshire weather and, of course, the changing of the leaves. There is something bittersweet about this seasonal "passion play" that presents such a beautiful palette of colors and yet at the same time also signifies death and the coming of winter. It was at the height of this season, which in the Carolinas can be fleeting, that Yogi and I began meeting every Friday for lunch at Southern Roots, our favorite High Point eatery.

The food is amazing at Southern Roots, and the atmosphere is casual and relaxed. Perhaps the greatest attraction for Yogi was that the Adams Inn, where the restaurant was located, often hosted weekend weddings, and almost every Friday the restaurant was overrun with beautiful young women gathering to celebrate the nuptials of a dear friend. Of course, the young ladies were gorgeous, but I think it was something more that made them so appealing to Yogi. Perhaps it was their vibrant spirits, the excitement of the event, or the expectation and the promise of new beginnings. To this day, I have vivid memories of those afternoons. I can still smell the intoxicating aromas of food that would engulf us the moment we arrived, the meals we ate to excess, the beautiful scenery and, most of all, the love that always flowed from Yogi's side of the table to mine.

Our initial thought concerning those Friday lunches was to talk about Yogi's life so that his eulogy would be a true picture of my friend's life, loves and innermost thoughts. Like most of the discussions Yogi and I shared over the years, this first one was an intentional and focused look at the very heart of his beliefs.

As one of the most spiritually introspective and intentional men I have ever known, Yogi believed that an unexamined life was a wasted life, and he went to great lengths to live a life of contemplation, prayer, purpose and action. He told me about the many times over the years when he had gone away for a few days of solitude, prayer, planning and listening for God's voice. It was clear that understanding what God intended for his life was at the very core of Yogi's heart and soul. He believed that a man's actions should always reflect his inner beliefs, and these beliefs were what he shared with me that first day of our journey.

On that particular day, my life was like most of my fellow baby boomers: two very active teenagers at home, my wife and I both working in busy and fulfilling careers, coaching club soccer, volunteering with Young Life, active at church, engaged in the local community and involved in a thousand other obligations that often left me wondering if there were any truly contemplative or intentional thoughts, much less actions in my life at all. At times, it seemed that I simply scurried from one obligation to the next with little opportunity for introspection and even less time for listening to what God might be trying to tell me about His plan for my life and the lives of my loved ones. I would soon learn that God did, indeed, have plenty to say to me. Sitting across the lunch table from Yogi that afternoon, I could feel the groundwork of a more durable spiritual foundation for my life beginning to form. I sensed that this gentle man would be the catalyst that would guide me to this path, and yet he was dying, literally, right before my eyes.

Yogi believed that there were a few very simple yet profound principals that govern the well-lived life. He believed that God provided life lessons to keep us grounded and focused on the truly important gifts of life. As Yogi dug into his burger, he began ruminating upon the first of his life-centering principles, something he liked to call his "joy conundrum."

He began unraveling the mystery of the joy conundrum for me by saying that so many people today buy into the three lies about joy that the world would have us believe: first, that joy comes from the acquisition of wealth; second, that happiness is determined by focusing on our own personal needs; and third, that self-contentment is ultimately derived from the attainment of power and influence.

Yogi discovered early that life's conditions don't have to dictate one's happiness. He was born the 11th of 12 children into a family not only poor and struggling materially, but also emotionally and spiritually. Poverty can break a person's spirit, and for a young man like Yogi who had often worn hand-me-down clothing, who lived in a house without indoor plumbing, and who was not, it seemed, destined to have many educational opportunities, growing up and growing bitter over his lot in life would have been an easy path to take. But Yogi deliberately chose not to live in a world of "me," mired and frustrated by his circumstances. He chose, instead, a higher and ultimately more fulfilling path.

Even as a child, Yogi recognized the importance of being part of a larger community, and he yearned to find his place in the world. He often mentioned that the single most impactful decision of his childhood years was when he joined, on his own, the Reeds Baptist Church. He often attended services on his own and rarely missed a meeting, for it was in this tiny country church that Yogi first experienced the joy of unconditional love and the warm embrace of a community.

His church family very quickly became a critically important lifeline for Yogi. At first he was almost shocked to learn that it mattered to them that he did not own a warm jacket for the upcoming winter or that his shoes had holes in the soles. They seemed anxious to make sure he always had what he needed, and this profoundly touched Yogi's heart. Through their display of generosity, grace and love, he learned not to be ashamed of his need, but instead to embrace the joy that can be experienced by both the giver and the recipient; this would be a life-changing lesson that would guide his philanthropy throughout his life.

As I listened to Yogi talk about his family's poverty, his early despair, and the many acts of compassion and thoughtfulness that had inundated his youth, I began to understand his insatiable desire to help others. I learned that the happiest and most content people Yogi had known throughout his life were those who had given freely of their time, their resources and most of all their affection, and Yogi had intentionally modeled his life after them.

From his early childhood until that day, Yogi had stayed true to these values. This mind-set was never more evident than on the day, about eight months before his death, when he and his dear friend Raymond Payne encountered two young boys during their daily stop at the downtown High Point Post Office.

Raymond is a gentle and almost regal African-American man who had also overcome more than his fair share of life's more difficult challenges. He had courageously climbed above his rage, self-contempt, addiction, incarceration and homelessness to become a tireless and effective advocate for the homeless in High Point through the Rabbit Quarter Ministry, an organization he established to help the disenfranchised in our community. With their shared dedication to and compassion for the hardcore homeless and downtrodden, it wasn't a surprise to anyone that Yogi and Raymond would meet and become fast friends. As they worked side by side serving meals to the homeless, they became so much more than friends; they became brothers.

Later, when Yogi's illness took a turn for the worse and he began to require more care than Martha could provide, it was Raymond who stepped in and became his constant companion and caregiver. They shared an unspoken chemistry, accentuated by a lively ongoing banter. This tall, handsome African-American man and a short, chubby white guy in his "pimped out" wheelchair made a most unusual couple. Their lively conversations were an ongoing comedy routine that entertained anyone within earshot. Yet, the love and respect they shared crossed all boundaries of race, culture and economics. They truly and unashamedly loved one another.

So, on that sunny day outside the post office, Yogi was zipping around in his wheelchair and Raymond was walking beside him carrying his mail when they encountered two young African-American boys sprawled upon the grass right in front of Yogi's van. Yogi called out and asked them how things were going. In the brief encounter that followed, Yogi and Raymond learned that the boys played football at the local high school, were being raised by a single mom and were about to start school, which neither appeared to be too excited about.

Yogi, the lifelong student and ardent lover of teachers, immediately asked the boys why in the world they weren't excited about returning to school. The question struck a chord and the boys fell silent. It was readily apparent that the reason was much deeper than the usual laments of being cooped up inside all day, having too much homework and too many tests. Yogi studied the boys for a moment then casually asked if they had been shopping for school clothes yet. Both boys grew restless, and with downcast eyes the older one softly told Yogi that there wasn't money for new clothes this year. Yogi was now on familiar ground. Without missing a beat, or sounding patronizing, he informed the boys that "We would just have to do something about that." He immediately turned to Raymond and informed him that they were changing the day's itinerary and would be taking these young men school shopping. "After all," he reminded them, "you've got to look sharp on your first day of school."

In the adventure that followed, I am absolutely sure that no one had more fun than Yogi. In between the ice cream, the joking around and the many purchases, he likely recalled a time when he had gone without nice clothes. He remembered those wonderful people at Reeds Baptist Church who had always made sure he looked good on the first day of school, and who, with their love, affection and dreams for a young boy, had prepared him to one day pass on this blessing.

Amid the chatter of conversations taking place in the Southern Roots dining room that day, the memory of helping those two young men brought a smile to Yogi's face. I watched my friend quietly revel in the momentary bliss that always comes when we shift the focus from ourselves and onto others. As he began to speak, I knew he was still caught in a distant moment outside the post office on the beautiful sunny day as he joked with Raymond and watched his new young friends strut around in their just purchased school clothes. I could only imagine the sweetness of the memory and how this unselfish act of "loving on" those two boys had created a memory that sustained him even now in his time of need when life's challenges were rapidly becoming so much harder to bear.

During the entire 16 months of his final journey, not once did I see Yogi angry or outwardly sad about his situation. I've often wondered how he could have been so calm about facing his own mortality. I remember asking him if there were dark moments in which he felt rage at the terrible hand he had been dealt? He responded to me in a classic Yogi Yarborough manner by shaking his head and smiling even more broadly. He told me that life was not about being happy; he said that was another lie the world would have us believe. He explained that what life was really about was being of use, serving others and living in such a way that we create good and lasting memories, memories that would sustain us through the storms of life that would inevitably come. Memories like the one he had created with those two boys at the post office so many months before on a balmy Carolina afternoon that now lived on forever. He went on to remind me that joy was always a self-inflicted wound that finds us only when we choose to look beyond ourselves.

Yogi closed his eyes and took a deep breath and I could tell he was tiring. I motioned to the waiter for our check, and as we prepared to leave, I realized that despite the deadlines, the pressures at work and the inevitable struggles and disappointments, life really was pretty wonderful. I promised myself that when I got home that night I would hug my little boy, Jordie; kiss my daughter, Taylor; and tell my wife how beautiful she was, because this was the day I'd learned that joy, real joy, is where you choose to find it.

CHAPTER 3

THE GIFT OF SUFFERING

UNDERSTANDING THAT OUR MOST PROFOUND
GROWTH COMES THROUGH ADVERSITY AND LIKE
THE SCULPTOR'S CHISEL, IT IS THE STRUGGLE THAT
SHAPES US INTO WHO WE WERE CREATED TO BE

"God will not look you over for medals,

degrees or diplomas, but for scars."

~ Elbert Hubbard

It was a couple of months into our Friday lunch routine that I found myself watching Yogi deftly navigate his wheelchair around the linen covered tables of a somewhat rowdy Southern Roots lunch crowd. Yogi and I had become fixtures at the restaurant by this time; all the waitresses knew us by name and were great about helping Yogi with his increasing physical needs. In the soft blush of an autumn noon sun I could see the deepening lines of fatigue on my friend's face, lines that I knew ALS was carving in its own cruelly measured pace. Yet, there was Yogi, ever smiling as if in open defiance of the disease, employing every fiber of his being to move forward, always like a determined athlete pushing away the steely fingers of fatigue by sheer power of will.

It was this image and the appreciation of my friend's perseverance that led us to our topic of discussion that day, "the art of suffering well." As always, we exchanged greetings while Yogi began his assault on a huge plate of okra, pinto beans and fried chicken. He was nearly halfway through his meal when he abruptly looked up and announced that he believed that God uses the gift of suffering to teach each of us what is most important in life. He went on to explain how all of the most significant insights in his life had been the direct result of suffering. Why is it, he wondered, that we all work so "doggone" hard to avoid that which makes us better?

I was still working on my salad as I tried to digest this newest nugget of wisdom Yogi had just tossed my way. I thought back over the hard experiences of my life and it wasn't long before I could see the pattern of suffering throughout my life journey leading to insight. There was the childhood spent moving from place to place and the struggle to make friends and gain acceptance in every new Marine base we moved to. Then I recalled the monumental struggle I encountered during my early years of school trying desperately to learn how to read and the constant sense of failure and stupidity that learning disabilities fostered. How could I forget my sophomore year in college when I had spent the previous summer serving with the Marines instead of playing summer soccer league and the fall season that followed in which I saw more of the bench then the field?

Each of these experiences was still vividly etched in my mind and while the pain had for the most part receded, the lessons learned had not. The nomadic lifestyle of my youth had taught me to be adaptable and proactive when it came to relationships. The struggle with reading was a tough one and since this had taken place before we knew anything about "learning disabilities" outliving the stigma of being lazy or simply stupid had taken years. Yet, the work my mother and I invested into conquering my reading disabilities had forged a love relationship that had only grown stronger over the years and greatly impacted my parenting in a very positive way. I also developed a passion for reading that led to reading a book-a-week habit to this day, a double major of History and English in college, graduate school, post graduate work at Harvard University and a successful career as a writer and speaker.

Finally, my college sophomore soccer curse had been a real challenge for me, as I had started right from the start my freshman year and defined myself through my athletics up to that point in my life. That year taught me that I was so much more than just soccer. I also learned that serving my country had certainly been worth one year of college soccer and most of all, I had developed leadership skills through the Marine Corps that came in handy during my senior year when I served as one of the captains of the team.

Of course, Yogi was right, as he normally was when he shared his insights into life through mouthfuls of okra and beans. There was much to be learned in the angst and disappointment that always accompanies genuine suffering. He was also spot-on when he noted that suffering was the gift all of us need but none of us want. He had certainly aroused my interest and I couldn't help but ask him why he thought God designed it that way.

I watched Yogi push back from his immaculate plate, gingerly wipe the remnants of lunch from his chin and settle his gaze squarely upon me. A sad smile crossed his lips as he began to tell me about how, several years ago, he had suffered a complete nervous breakdown. With a light in his eyes that could only come from the deepest conviction, he explained that this dark chapter, as bad as it had been, had taught him how absolutely precious the gift of life really is.

He said that struggling with an unrelenting and heartless opponent like depression had taught him so much about the true nobility of suffering well, and he assured me that his breakdown, with its veil of utter hopelessness, had been far more horrible than cancer, or ALS, could ever be.

Breakdowns always seem to happen at totally inconvenient times, and it was no different in Yogi's case. It had been during one of the most successful periods of his professional career that this creeping blackness had slipped in to take hold of his life. His business was thriving, his family was growing, and yet he could not seem, no matter how hard he tried, to fight back the darkness that was gradually taking over his life. While Yogi had never liked to dwell on the negative, he did say that his depression had been the product of emotional demons from his past that he had never really taken the time to overcome; he had always been too busy. He recalled the loneliness and poverty of his youth, the despair that had followed him throughout his high school and the disappointments and setbacks that occurred during his college years that had led to his first bout with depression. He knew that the origins of this darkness were directly related to his desperate longing to be special, his overwhelming desire to be successful and most of all, his lifelong quest for intimacy and love.

Suddenly in the midst of prosperity and success, the icy breath of depression had caught up with him once again without premonition or warning. Eventually, the ever present, always increasing weight of despair overwhelmed him at work, then at home and finally Yogi ended up being hospitalized. During those long weeks of isolation in the hospital the emotional ache he felt from being separated from his wife and sons soon matched the constant pain of the depression itself. He recalled how he would literally try to submerge himself in the late afternoon shadows and weep for the sound of his family's voices and the feel of their touch.

In the end, he decided that it had been a crisis of faith and he told me it only ended after he had finally come to grips with what he knew had been a battle for his heart that could never be soothed by achievement, wealth or fame. He discovered in the midst of this struggle that his faith in God and his belief in the sacred refuge that only the Holy Spirit could provide were enough to sustain him on his journey back to his family. He realized that over the years he had worked so hard, had kept so busy and focused, that he had never taken the time, or the risk, to see how much God really did love him just as he was. Yogi had finally gotten his arms around the fact that the millions of dollars, the cars, trips, homes, good works and recognitions could never assuage the hurt of a lonely boy who had simply wanted to be loved.

Yogi blinked hard as if to pull himself back into the warm Friday afternoon. As our eyes met, he could see that I was crying. He told me that yes; absolutely yes, he would choose cancer and ALS over depression every single day of the week. He reasoned that at least with cancer and ALS you had foes that can be seen and grappled with. Depression had been different, for it cuts so deeply into one's soul and lays siege upon one's heart. He then told me that he knew his depression was over when he could finally hear God's voice rise above all the dark and angry voices that had crowded his heart all those years. It was the same voice, the voice of a loving and faithful God that was leading him now and this had been the gift of his suffering. He winked as he told me that he was going to be all right, no matter what happened in the coming months which we both knew would be difficult beyond measure, so long as he could continue to hear God's reassuring voice.

It was on that day that I finally understood that suffering is a most essential gift for all of us. It is the struggle none of us desire and yet it is the "severe mercy" all of us so desperately need. I could now see that suffering is the chisel with which God shapes us into the men and women He created us to be. There was enormous strength in the knowledge that the Creator of the Universe had cared so much for Yogi that He was willing to grapple with him for so long, just as He had done hundreds of years ago with Jacob, to make him whole and complete. It was that knowledge, I believe, that got Yogi out of that hospital, over the depression, and finally back to his family. Suffering would never look or feel the same to me again...

CHAPTER 4

FAMILY...
THE GREATEST ADVENTURE OF ALL

DISCOVERING THAT OUR MOST PROFOUND BLESSINGS
ARE FOUND IN THE LOVE, CHAOS, JOY, DEBRIS,
FULFILLMENT AND INTIMACY THAT IS A FAMILY

"A man travels the world over in search of what he needs
and returns home to find it."

~ George Augustus Moore

Family can be the most intimate and sacred of all relationships. It can also be messy, heart-wrenching, frustrating, traumatic and, at times, humiliating. At the end of the day, family is undoubtedly worth the struggle, for it is they who truly see into our hearts and souls, who speak the hard truths and who work in tandem with God in the never-ending process of shaping us into the men and women God created us to be.

During one of the most challenging times in my life, it was my family that sustained me and ultimately saved me from leaping over the edge. I have learned over the years that there are distinct seasons in our lives in which mysteriously powerful forces seem to conspire to push us to what we think is the very threshold of our tolerance. These overwhelming, converging circumstances almost appear to be driven by the primordial tides and phases of the moon. For some, these experiences encompass days; for me, the entire year of 2005 will go down as my "season of despair," a span of time that pushed me nearly to the utter reaches of endurance and hope. It was an episode in which patience ceased to be just a virtue and gradually became a tenuous lifeline that barely saved me from falling off into the darkest abyss.

The essential ingredients of my "dark days" included a vaguely written city noise ordinance, an elderly empty-nesting couple who shared curiously neurotic noise and control issues, the adjustment to the perils of menopause, my beloved son's mission to set a new demerit speed record at his school, and my beautiful, amazingly strong-willed 17-year-old daughter's year of living dangerously with what can only be described as the stereotypical boyfriend from hell.

Looking back, it is almost humorous, like one of those outrageous family comedies that always seem to launch endless sequels in which the beaten down, beleaguered father ultimately gets bailed out of jail, reunited with his family and cautiously reinstated with the civilized world by forces both seen and unseen. However, the repressed memories of that year make me shudder even to this day.

It was in the midst of this emotionally precarious year that I found myself settling into the routine of my weekly Friday lunches with Yogi. Having grown up as a Marine Corps brat who had never lived anywhere longer than a couple years, I had come to appreciate the intimacy and familiarity of sustained friendships. I often marveled at how long I had known Yogi.

If there was ever a man who adored his family, it was Yogi. He considered his wife Martha and his boys, Scott and Preston, to be gifts from his God, unexpected miracles, and he could rarely talk of them without breaking out in a helpless grin.

I clearly remember Yogi the first time we met. He was walking Preston and Scott up to the soccer camp registration table, one on each side of him resolutely holding his hands with no intention of letting go. Unlike most of the kids who attended the camp, Yogi's boys didn't get picked up by one of the countless "soccer moms" whose minivans overran our field house each day. While Martha was a devoted mother who doted on her sons, it was Yogi who collected the boys at camp every day, and it was plain to see that was not a chore, but instead a privilege that brought him great joy.

Yogi owned a thriving furniture hardware business, and I remember thinking that it must have been a real challenge for him to break away so early in the afternoon to watch his boys flying around the soccer field. But day after day, there he was. It was obvious that Yogi wanted to be nowhere at that moment other than on the field watching his boys play. He followed their every move with a sense of joy and enthusiasm that clearly conveyed an old athlete's appreciation for physical competition and a father's unconditional love for his boys. His eyes always told me that those boys were his "pearls of great value," his treasures on earth.

Yogi never knew he was being so closely watched. He was simply following his heart and loving his boys the only way he knew how, with total and utter abandonment. Yet after 30 years, I still remember the look of pure, unadulterated joy that radiated from his face as he watched his boys. That look profoundly touched me. It was a look of passion, one that had inspired me years later to strive to be the same kind of father to my son and daughter. It's ironic. Even before I really knew Yogi, he was already teaching me the inherent value of family and the importance of appreciating this incredible gift every single moment. What I loved most about Yogi was that throughout his life he always instructed in the way of the very best teachers – by personal example.

So on this particular rainy Friday afternoon at Southern Roots, Yogi initiated our discussion by asking how my family was doing. Reluctantly at first, I began sharing a litany of doubts and fears revolving around my most recent attempts at fathering and husbanding. Yogi sat back and let me ramble on as he began to methodically attack the vegetable plate lying before him.

As my tirade was winding down, Yogi was polishing off his final piece of cornbread, which he had carefully used to clean up the remaining gravy from his plate. After a few seconds of silence, he finally asked if I ever wondered what my life would have been like had I never married my wife, fathered my two children and acquired the menagerie of pets with which we had shared our home over the years.

I paused, conjuring up images of a perfectly organized home, a bathroom without towels, underwear and cosmetics strewn about haphazardly, an uncluttered and unhurried schedule, and long quiet nights spent reading … all by myself. I saw myself in a perfect home where I lived in splendid isolation … and knew immediately that it was an antiseptic vision of a perfectly incomplete life.

Yogi grinned as he observed my silent ruminations; then he began to speak in his raspy, nonjudgmental tone. He told me that he believed that family is God's way of showing us that we are all inherently incomplete, that we are, at best, stumbling, constantly evolving "works in progress." He told me that our families are indeed the highest calling of our earthly life as they inspire our highest virtues, reveal our deepest failings and reinforce the desire to know that we are loved and are actually capable of returning that love.

Yogi paused, lost in his reflections of his own life of struggle and reward. I knew the story of his childhood, and I could only imagine the incredible challenges he had to maneuver around to reach his goals.

Over 40 years ago, Yogi had overcome impossible odds just to attend college, much less graduate. Few who had known him as a child could have believed that he would ever earn a degree, yet he had achieved this goal and was preparing to dive head first into his business career. He had also recently met a beautiful young woman named Martha Huggin, the daughter of one of High Point's most prominent ministers. For Yogi, it had been love at first sight.

Martha was, and still is, a beautiful, petite redhead who seemed to embody everything Yogi had ever wanted in a wife. She was bright, independent, hardworking, passionate about life and, thankfully, just a bit shorter than he. They met on a blind date, and right away, Yogi approached the courtship with his typical determination and focused energy. Martha saw his sincerity and vulnerability immediately, which only made her love him more. She admired the pure and honest effort he put into everything he did, but most of all she loved the effort he put into courting her. Within a year, they were engaged and ready to start a life together. The bliss would not last long.

As was customary in the '60s, the soon-to-be bride and groom visited local doctors for physical examinations before applying for a marriage license. It was during his visit to the doctor that Yogi's carefully planned life suddenly came apart at the seams. The exam revealed a suspicious lump on one of his testicles, which, upon closer examination, was confirmed to be a cancerous tumor. This particular form of the disease was the same type of virulent cancer that had taken the life of Chicago Bears' star running back Brian Piccolo, who would later be immortalized in the film, *Brian's Song*.

As you would expect, Yogi's diagnosis was devastating, as testicular cancer was at that time a real man killer that medicine had yet to conquer. Any kind of cancer had a grim prognosis back then, and Yogi's doctor was blunt in his assessment — he was not optimistic.

To say he and Martha were devastated could only be described as a tragic understatement. In a split second, the energy, optimism and momentum he had generated after such an unprecedented climb out of poverty was tragically and suddenly stilled.

After much discussion and insistence on Yogi's part, the wedding was promptly postponed. Yogi was immediately scheduled for surgery, which was followed by several weeks of excruciating cobalt radiation, a brutal therapy that left him with terrible sores, overwhelming fatigue and lifelong scars.

The radiological full-court press all but ensured that Yogi would never father children. He and his beautiful bride had enthusiastically talked about children from the very beginning of their relationship and longed to start a family. Their dream, or at least this part of it, seemed to be over.

Being the honorable man that he was, Yogi gave Martha every opportunity to walk away; after all, having children had been so important to her. But Martha saw in Yogi the strength and goodness she wanted, and she believed in their love. She committed herself to whatever the future held for the two of them. Yogi saw this as a divine confirmation that he had been truly blessed; that Martha was indeed the woman he had always longed for. She was a wife who would love and believe in him, who would always be in his corner, the soul mate he had been searching for his entire life.

Winning a war when you're the decided underdog takes time and energy, yet being the fighter that he was, Yogi bravely battled his way through the nightmare with Martha at his side. Within two years, the doctors pronounced that he was healed of his cancer; Yogi had defied the odds once again.

Yogi and Martha married in High Point and honeymooned in Bermuda. While elated and relieved that the cancer was gone, there was a distant realization that they had both lost something of incalculable value. While it was never stated out loud, they both grieved and worked to accept that they might never experience the joys of parenthood.

Yogi's rapidly growing business, an active social life and the excitement of a new marriage kept them busy and fulfilled. The yawning void that a future without children cast was always with them, but still absent from conversation. However, an undeterred Yogi, who knew just a little bit about achieving the impossible, continued to pray every single night that God might intercede and give them the children they longed for.

Despite the scars from his illness, the effects of the radiation, his brush with death, Yogi continued to walk by faith and not by sight. He always believed in his heart that he would one day be blessed with children. He prayed with the innocence and blind confidence of a child, and when the day came that Martha joyfully and tearfully announced that that he was going to be a father, Yogi wasn't as much surprised as he was grateful. Life had taught him long ago that the God he loved was always looking out for him, always listening and always full of surprises.

His two boys, Preston and Scott, the little soccer players he came to watch each day with such complete joy and appreciation, grew up to be remarkable young men who love with the same sincerity and passion as their father. To Preston, the athlete, Yogi imparted his amazing speed, competitive drive, a lifelong love of books and a passion for godly wisdom. To Scott, the businessman, Yogi gave wisdom, a strong work ethic, energy, and a deep and abiding love for the New York Mets, who years later they would watch together at Shea Stadium as they won the World Series. All three men shared a passion for prayer, an unwaivering faith in the dependability of God, and a desire to help those less fortunate.

Yogi was fond of what he called the "God moments" with his boys, those times when he said their "souls met." He told me that it was in the midst of these times with his boys that the true value of God's amazing healing miracle was made complete. These boys, unexpected gifts, were loved and nurtured by a grateful man who understood that a man's greatest contributions in life are loving his wife well and leaving behind a new generation who understands and appreciates the miraculous nature of God.

Yogi leaned back in his chair and smiled. I could see that he was tiring. He told me, without hesitation or reservation, that he was a man who had been blessed far beyond his wildest dreams. He said it had nothing to do with the many millions he had made, his beautiful homes, his public recognitions or his many other successes.

He was blessed because through it all, in the good times and the bad, he had been able to count on the love of his family. Yogi knew, without doubt, that there were three people who always believed in him, counted on him and trusted him to be the father and the husband that God had created him to be.

In that moment, I realized that what may, at first, look like a long, frustrating "forced march" can sometimes be the most beautiful dance of all ... the privilege of walking arm in arm with those you love through life's uncharted territory knowing that you have freely given your heart, and in turn, have been truly and completely loved ... no matter what.

CHAPTER 5

GOD, FAITH AND TOOTSIE POPS

UNDERSTANDING THAT FREEDOM IS THE
ABSOLUTELY TERRIFYING ACT OF WALKING BY FAITH
AND NOT BY SIGHT

"Now faith is the substance of things hoped for,

the evidence of things not seen."

~ Hebrews 11:1

It was midway through what had become a relatively mild North Carolina winter that I began to realize just how much the time I had been spending with Yogi was changing my life. Our conversations were altering my perception of faith and teaching me to be a more loving father and nurturing husband.

I had begun to realize that when my life was busy, it became easy to simply go with the flow, like a kayaker who sits back and allows the current to simply pull him down river. Sunday morning services, Wednesday night services and Sunday school classes were wonderful, but like many things in the rhythm of life, they can sometimes lull our souls to sleep. We can be physically present in all sorts of religious activities, yet spiritually absent in our faith.

It is often said that one does not fully appreciate the physical and spiritual freedom that comes with good health until it is threatened. As I watched my friend systematically losing little pieces of his life, I was beginning to understand just how fragile life really is and how none of us should take it for granted.

Yogi's illness continued its grim progression, and at each step I felt my heart break a little bit more. Every new development was ushered in with the appearance of an insidious advanced guard, sometimes it was an ache, other times it was a loss of feeling, or the tell-tale sign, a tingling sensation. Then the weakness arrived. The disease had begun in his right leg first, then the left. Soon each of his arms began to be affected. It was an utterly helpless feeling to watch my friend gradually being stripped of his strength, his mobility and, ultimately, his independence. What amazed me most about this process was that I never saw fear or anger in the man. Instead, I watched him grow more peaceful, more accepting and even more joyful. Watching him deal with these profound losses opened my eyes as never before to the incredible breadth of God's unrelenting grace.

My friend Yogi believed that faith was very simple; it was about building, sustaining and sharing an intimate and vibrant relationship with his Creator, period. It was about walking, talking, worshiping, crying, loving, arguing with, listening to, struggling and reaching out to his God who was with each passing day becoming his very best friend and closest confidant.

Each week at lunch, I would catch myself looking for any changes, sometimes small, sometimes dramatic, in Yogi's physical condition. One week he was just really tired; another, he had breathing problems; and sometimes he was simply discovering another loss in his range of motion. One thing that never changed throughout the entire journey was his attitude. Yogi didn't believe in wasting a single minute feeling sorry for himself; he abhorred self-pity.

I can still hear Yogi talking about the people who asked if he was angry at God; wanting to know if he questioned why it was him and not someone else who had received this cosmic slap in the face. His response was always the same; he would smile and sometimes even laugh when he gave his standard response, "Why not me?"

I think it was the many challenges he had faced throughout his life that endowed Yogi with such a strong sense of optimism. You might say that his steadfast belief in the unseen sustained him in good times and bad. On this particular Friday afternoon, I found Yogi basking in the warm noon sun that was pouring in through the windows that looked out over the Adams Inn courtyard. The sheer pleasure and contentment in the glow that engulfed him reminded me so much of my golden retriever, Stormy. She was a gentle, loving soul who was battling a particularly harsh cancer that had robbed her of her normal exuberance. These days, she liked nothing better than to simply lie in the sun with the same sense of serenity I could now see in Yogi's weary face. When I first sat down, Yogi kept his eyes closed, smiling and content as he slowly began to talk about God, faith and his steadfast belief in the sanctity of Tootsie Pops.

Yogi loved all foods, especially candy, but he always had a very special affinity for Tootsie Pops. He had become somewhat of a local legend with the kids in the community, as he never went anywhere without a pocket full of those Tootsie Pops that he would enthusiastically offer to any child who passed his way. He always said that he'd never had a bad one, never grew sick of them and that they always seemed to make people happy. In fact, Yogi used to tell me that Tootsie Pops were a lot like God. They were something you could depend on, a constant that always delivered. In the same way, Yogi knew he could never really have a bad day because no matter what he might be doing, or wherever he went, he knew God was always there for him. Just like in the 139th Psalm where we are reminded that, "He discerns my going out and my lying down; He is familiar with all my ways… If I rise on the wings of the dawn, if I settle on the far side of the sea, even there your hand will guide me; your right hand will hold me fast."

Yogi's faith taught him that while his circumstances might be grim at a particular moment, there would always be something in it that God could use for good. His life had little to do with having good or bad days; it was instead about his faith and his willingness to love others unconditionally, in the same way God loved him. This precept of faith made Yogi's life very simple. When he saw a child in pain, a mother in need, a man stripped of his dignity or self-worth, a junkie begging for money, a prostitute offering her body, a youngster lashing out in anger, or even a person of wealth and influence holding a sense of entitlement over others, he reached out to help because he believed we are the keepers of our brothers and sisters.

That day he told me a story about the woman who gave him the gift of faith that would sustain him in his ongoing struggle with ALS. The memory of this unforgettable woman made him smile as he closed his eyes and took a long breath. He began telling me the story about a woman who had nothing of value in the world's currency and yet was able to give Yogi the greatest gift of all.

Going back more than 20 years, while in his 30s, Yogi, by all accounts, seemed to have achieved the American dream. He owned a successful business and was a self-made millionaire. He had a beautiful home, a loving family and plenty of friends. He wore the nicest clothes, owned all the toys, sent his boys to the finest schools and drove a beautiful

Porsche convertible that cost more than most folks in Lexington made in a lifetime. Yet he frequently caught himself wondering if something was missing. He possessed everything he had ever dreamed of, yet he woke up every morning with a nagging realization that there was more out there and he wanted to find it. Ironically, it would be an old, impoverished, nearly blind, African-American woman who was about to save him from himself. Yogi met her by sheer chance one night when he was volunteering to deliver meals for shut-ins with Meals on Wheels in a rundown neighborhood on the south side of High Point. I remember being struck by the irony that this forgotten old woman would be the one who first recognized the depth of Yogi's spiritual poverty and who cared enough to show him what was missing in his life.

Her name was Mrs. Powers, and she was all alone in the world. The short span of life that lay ahead of her was punctuated by rapidly encroaching blindness, fragile health and devastating poverty. Yet, Mrs. Powers gave Yogi a remarkable gift, a "Tootsie Pop faith," that would radically change his life and become the foundation of the spiritual awakening that would, years later, be the rock he leaned on in his time of greatest need.

Mrs. Powers didn't impart this gift in the manner our world has come to expect to find great insight and wisdom, for Mrs. Powers was not an educated woman. Nor was she powerful, wealthy or influential. She was a woman whom our world had very much forgotten, cast off to the side where she could live out her days in quiet, impoverished anonymity.

This special gift was one that could only be given by the disenfranchised and forgotten, for it was the gift of beggars, lepers and crucified thieves. It was the gift of blind faith, a belief in the unseen, the kind of faith that allows someone on the brink of losing everything to clearly understand that it is only by losing it all that we can gain that which can never be taken away.

When Yogi first met Mrs. Powers, he immediately sensed there was something very different and compelling about this serene old woman. Before he knew it, he was checking in on her twice, sometimes three times, a week. When he would show up unannounced, she never seemed to be surprised. In fact, Yogi always sensed that she had somehow been expecting him. She would light up at his appearance and she hugged him in the way that only a loving mother can. They would then sit and talk about that which was most important in her life ... her faith.

Yogi was initially surprised by the familiarity and the ease with which they communicated; it was as if they had known one another all their lives. He saw how this old woman who possessed so little of what the world considered to be of value yet she seemed to have so much more peace than anyone he had ever known. Even in her poverty and despite her rapidly diminishing health, she was truly content, which was such a contrast to the world Yogi lived in. Most of all, she was passionately in love with this God who was figuratively and literally everything to her. Yogi found his time with her baffling, exhilarating, terrifying, and eventually liberating.

As their relationship grew, Yogi began to understand that authentic faith only comes to us when we are willing to let go of all those things the world has taught us we can't live without. "Lord, Lord," Mrs. Powers would say to Yogi. "Wherever your treasure lies, that's where your heart will always be."

Months passed. Yogi found himself spending more and more time sitting and praying with Mrs. Powers. He was captivated by her gratefulness at even the most insignificant things God passed her way. She delighted over the simple gifts: a warm day, a beautiful sunset, a prayer with Yogi's boys, a blossoming flower, a cooling breeze and most of all, the knowledge that she was significant in the life of this very special man. How strange it now seemed that Yogi had once almost pitied Mrs. Powers, this poor old woman who had no one and owned nothing. Yet now he felt privileged to be able to sit beside her and pray with her and he longed to be more like her so that he too could experience the peace she knew.

Mrs. Powers relied upon her Bible to answer most of Yogi's questions. She never pretended to be more than an old woman who was simply passing time until she "crossed over the river" to meet her God, her faithful companion, her husband who had so faithfully taken care of her over those many years. After all, wasn't it God who had brought her comfort and companionship during her final days by leading Yogi to her door?

Yogi's eyes would light up when he talked about the power of her prayers and how he used to love to take his boys to visit her. He wanted them to see what a true love relationship with God looked like. When she prayed, in her soft, humble way, Yogi said he could feel God's presence. He marveled at the power that this tiny little woman could summon by simply folding her hands and raising her eyes to heaven.

Yogi's transformation took time, as there were always other urgent voices competing for his heart. Like many, Yogi's life was often determined by the urgency of the moment and the responsibilities he believed dictated his daily itinerary. After all, he was a very successful man at the top of his game; it was easy for him to believe that he was the one who was actually in charge.

This misconception was routinely reinforced by the prestige and excitement of his corporate success, the increasing influence he could wield as a highly respected community leader, his steadily growing wealth and the pride he took in his possessions, the kind of satisfaction that only those raised in poverty could understand. There were also the legitimate demands of a young family. For so many years, Yogi had been holding on for dear life, clutching all of these cherished possessions tightly in a clenched fist instead of holding them gently in the open palm of his hand.

The more time Yogi spent with Mrs. Powers, the more he relaxed his grip on his earthly treasures. This, in turn, softened his heart and made him more willing to trust God's love and protection. It also helped him accept that the God of the Universe could passionately desire to embrace and pursue a lonely boy like him who had only ever wanted to be special and loved.

As the weeks turned into months, Yogi began to experience a lifting of his burden and a calming sense of contentment that comes from the knowledge of being loved and cherished by a Father who will never forsake him. This simple gift of faith was so precious to Yogi because it was being passed on to him not by a member of the clergy or an educated Bible scholar, but instead through the humility and grace of this old, impoverished woman's heart for God.

It was during a business trip that Yogi first learned that Mrs. Powers' condition had taken a dramatic turn for the worse. He immediately cancelled his appointments and flew home to find her looking fragile and small amidst the quilts of her tiny single bed. She smiled as he sat beside her, and just as Yogi had reached out to hold my hand at the restaurant, Mrs. Powers reached out for his. She coughed weakly and cleared her throat before she began to speak. She told my friend that she was dying and assured him it was okay. She told him she was ready to cross the River Jordan where she would be reunited with her God, her heavenly father who had been her constant source of strength during the autumn years of her life.

Her only regret was that she would be leaving behind her dear friend, Yogi, whom she believed God had so faithfully provided to be her comfort and joy in the final season of her life. Amidst his tears, Mrs. Powers gave Yogi one final gift, one he would treasure for the rest of his life. She asked him to sit at her funeral as her son, the son she never had, whom God had blessed her with at a time when she so desperately needed a sign of His faithfulness.

Faith, blind and absolute, was the gift she wanted to bequeath to her son, her Yogi. As she gazed into his tear-filled eyes, she knew her gift to him was complete and that henceforth his life would never be the same. Mrs. Powers died two days later. As she had requested, Yogi sat as her son at the sparsely attended funeral for the tiny, seemingly insignificant woman who had been blessed with the greatest gift of all. Mrs. Powers had forever changed the life of a man who had accumulated everything our world had to offer by teaching him that "he is no fool who gives what he cannot keep, to gain what he cannot lose."

As Yogi listened to the minister speak of her life and her remarkable faith, he knew that Mrs. Powers had already crossed over the river and she was reunited with the God she had loved and served so well. He considered the magnitude of the gift of faith which she had passed on to him in that sad little "shotgun" house in one of the most impoverished neighborhoods in High Point. He had to smile, for he now knew that it had always been his pride, his determination and his insatiable drive that had deprived him of the peace he had so desperately wanted.

When Yogi finished his story, I saw him smile through the tears and the fatigue as he remembered his spiritual mother. She had been the one who had made God become real and relevant. It was that faith that now enabled Yogi to live life one day at a time and walk boldly in the face of his unspeakable disease. She had taught him the lesson that he now passed on to me: that a well-lived life is simply walking by faith and not by sight. This leap of faith is the only thing that will see us through the inevitable struggle, the pain and anguish of loss, and even to the final passage from this life to the next.

This was the day I knew Yogi was going to be all right. I knew that no matter where this illness took us in the months ahead, it would be OK. I realized, too, that just as Mrs. Powers had done for Yogi as she was dying, Yogi was now teaching me that the answer to the madness we call life is a free gift that God offers to each of us ... if only we would simply ask.

CHAPTER 6

LESSONS IN LOSING

DISCOVERING THAT SUCCEEDING ON THE FIRST
ATTEMPT SELDOM TEACHES OR INSPIRES LIKE FALLING
FLAT ON YOUR FACE

"Ah, but a man's reach should exceed his grasp,
or what's a heaven for?"

~ Robert Browning

Just like those Tootsie Pops my friend Yogi always loved so much, God never fails to deliver, never lets us down and never disappoints. My father, "The Colonel," was not always the most politically correct parent on the block. So it didn't surprise me when he took me aside one day and lovingly informed me that while I was a great kid with many fine attributes, I was not, and never would be, the sharpest tool in the metaphorical shed.

At first blush, this fraternal disclosure appeared harsh. Over the years, however, I came to see it as a good Marine's act of economy. The Colonel was always honest, and that day he went on to inform me that the Lessard men, who, up to that point, had never attended college, have always made up for their deficiencies with hard work, determination and an undying willingness to always rally back from defeat.

My elementary and junior high school teachers would no doubt have agreed with the Colonel's assessment, for I struggled mightily in my early years of school. After all I was a Marine Corps "brat" whose childhood had been spent moving from one duty station to the next throughout the world. By my senior year, I had attended 15 schools, and my nomadic lifestyle hadn't lent itself to the establishment of a solid academic foundation. It did, however, make me very adaptable socially as well as earning me an annual enrollment in various summer school programs around the country. Along the way, I came to agree with the Colonel that success in life is seldom based on one's innate talents, or raw potential. I learned that a truly significant life was all about pursuing that which is fair, right and just, without fear of failure, and when, not if, you fail, embracing a sincere commitment to dust yourself off and immediately jump back into the battle.

In an attempt to rise above my challenges, I determined early on that I would simply outwork my contemporaries to become a competitive athlete, a strong and enlightened reader, and lifelong learner. Having been diagnosed with learning disabilities, I soon discovered that reading was not going to be a skill that I would easily master. However, I had learned early on that reading well was one of those nonnegotiable prerequisites for success in any field. So while it took a considerable amount of time and a lot of patience on my part, I not only learned to be a competent reader, I soon fell in love with the idea of learning thanks to my parents' endless encouragement and dogged coaching.

Along the way there were a few spectacular "face plants" that helped me to remain humble and honest. However, by my senior year, things were coming together on both the scholastic and athletic fronts. I was named to the North Carolina High School All-Region and All-State soccer teams, which opened the door for a soccer/academic scholarship at High Point College. My acceptance into college was a real affirmation for me, as it confirmed in my mind that my hard work was paying off and I was indeed rising to my true potential.

It was during my senior year at Camp Lejeune High School that I first met Dani Lyttle, a young lady who would later prove to be one of the most defining influences in my life. While I didn't see it at the time, Dani would become one of the few friends from my childhood years whom I would actually be able to recall later in life and even keep up with. She turned out to be a real inspiration for what would become the next chapter of my academic life.

The oldest daughter of a Marine Lt. Colonel, Dani was a military vagabond like me. The difference between us was that she was a truly remarkable student and a naturally gifted writer. Together, she and I made our way with fear and trepidation through a very challenging Advanced Placement English class that was taught by a fabulous teacher named Dr. Ball.

Dr. Ball was a remarkable lady who possessed an uncanny resemblance to the Olive Oyl character from the old Popeye the Sailor cartoons. She had the wisdom of Yoda, the patience of Job and the heart of a well-trained assassin when she wielded her infamous red marker. I survived her class only through the remarkable mentoring and tutoring skills of my friend and fellow sojourner.

In every sense of the word, Dani was a "natural." At 17 years of age, she already possessed what Dr. Ball so seductively described as a "writer's voice." What set her apart even further was that she not only possessed the gift, she was willing to share it with us mortals who were not even worthy to sharpen her pencils. I remember thinking during one of our informal tutoring sessions that for Dani to share the secrets of her writing process with me was akin to Picasso teaching pre-school children how to finger paint.

True to my father's marching orders, I was determined, passionate and ready to fight to the bitter end. By the middle of my senior year, to my absolute amazement, Dr. Ball and Dani had transformed me into a competent, though still evolving, journeyman writer. Looking back, I don't know who enjoyed this journey more, for Dani seemed to take great joy, and I think at times sheer amusement, in the startling metamorphosis that was taking place right before her eyes.

Even she could not have imagined that this struggling caterpillar who had been kicking so hard just to stay afloat in AP English class would one day go on to major in English, earn a MFA in Communications, do post-graduate work at Harvard, and subsequently embark upon a career in which his ability to write and communicate would play a pivotal role in his ultimate professional success.

Years later as I climbed the steps of the Adams Inn to meet Yogi for lunch, my mood matched the darkened February skies, for just that morning I had learned that my old classmate and inspiration had been diagnosed with lung cancer. The inequity and random nature of this deadly illness infuriated me. Dani was a talented and loving wife, a mother of two teenage boys and a beloved school librarian who had never smoked a day in her life and suddenly without any reasonable explanation she found herself caught up in the fight of her life. I numbly navigated the lobby of the Adams Inn and made my way into the dining area as words like chemotherapy, biopsy, small cell carcinoma and life expectancy crowded my grief-stricken mind.

Yogi, as always, was flirting with the latest cast of the ongoing parade of brides and bridesmaids who so often lent such a welcomed feminine touch to our Friday lunch dates. I couldn't help but grin as I watched my friend charm the young ladies with his down-home mannerisms and genuine appreciation for the beauty and guiles of these beautiful southern women. Knowing that I was unashamedly predictable in my food preferences, Yogi had taken the liberty of ordering for us both. Having shared lunch with me over those many months, Yogi could never quite understand why, with all the amazing dishes offered in the Southern Roots menu, I would always order the same salad with the same sides and top it off with the same big glass of sweet tea. Yet it was comforting to know that Yogi knew me that well and I quietly marveled at how the sweet familiarity of friendship can sneak up on us at the strangest times.

After a brief update on work and family, I mentioned the news about Dani. To my complete surprise, and from somewhere deeply rooted in my soul, I let loose a single, very sloppy sob that startled us both. Yogi listened as I began to share my history with Dani. Being a cancer survivor himself, he took in every word, shared his hard-earned expertise and did his best to console me. He described the stark fear that accompanies the disease, the gut-wrenching fatigue that chemotherapy ushers in, and he noted that, in the end, the key to survival always comes down to one's willingness to fight and persevere.

Yogi knew a little bit about perseverance, and that day he spoke about a season of loss in his life that he believed had shaped him into the man he was on that day.

Like me, Yogi had been a lifelong and very passionate athlete. His natural athleticism was a true gift from God, for it ultimately provided the vehicle that would carry him away from the poverty of his youth. It was baseball that had defined him as a young boy. Playing the position of catcher, it seemed only natural that his nickname would come from another famous catcher, Yogi Berra.

As Yogi grew into his teenage years, football replaced baseball as his passion, and by high school, he had become one of the top running backs in the state. At a mere 5'4", Yogi's low center of gravity gave him the lethal gift of acceleration with the physical characteristics of a bowling ball, which made him very difficult to bring down. He had attracted the attention of area college coaches, and like several of his high school teammates, he found himself playing his first year of college ball at Wingate, a well-known incubator for future Atlantic Coast Conference football players.

During that first year, Yogi proved he could handle the school work and was talented enough to play at the collegiate level. He soon found himself headed to East Carolina University where he would get his chance to ply his skills in big-time arena of Southern college football.

The ECU coach had watched Yogi play at Wingate and had immediately liked what he saw; a tough, athletic young man who liked to hit and who ran with the sense of purpose and abandon that one only sees in those young men raised in poverty. He could plainly see that this Yarborough kid had a powerful need to prove himself. He also loved how Yogi had a natural, unrelenting desire to excel in every practice, every game, and every play. The coach wanted and needed brave hearts like Yogi on his team, for he knew their passion was contagious.

His coaches described Yogi as "scary quick," and they loved to watch him scamper to the open ground, a low-riding missile that even their 250-pound Clydesdales struggled to bring down. They could also see that the kid was pretty durable and seemed to be able to withstand the constant punishment of being hit by players twice his size.

What they admired most about Yogi, however, was that he never stayed down. No matter how hard he was hit, he always bounced up, complimented the hit and hustled back to the huddle. This was the kind of kid who could spark a program; this was a young man who made everyone around him better simply because he never surrendered. The coaching staff saw that Yogi's high expectations of himself were noticed by his teammates and that any team with lofty ambitions had to have inspirational leaders like him.

The coach had recognized and appreciated Yogi's character early on, and for that reason, he could not help but smile as he watched the young man step on the locker room scale after practice one afternoon. From his office vantage point on the far side of the locker room, the coach called out to his trainers to "not even think about measuring that Yarborough boy unless you can put a tape measure around his heart." Though brief and probably forgotten by most people in the room, the memory of that moment would become a source of strength and inspiration that Yogi would draw upon in the years to come.

As much as one might wish this football story would end happily, God had other plans for Yogi. During the middle of that first season at ECU, he sustained a very serious back injury that took him out for the season, required surgery and ultimately concluded with a bleak prognosis. In the blink of an eye, the gift of athleticism that had defined Yogi's life up to that point was gone forever. The suddenness and finality of the loss completely overwhelmed Yogi and left him wondering, if he could no longer be an athlete, who was he?

During the long days spent in the University infirmary, the only rays of hope that touched Yogi were the attentions of a kind nurse who "mothered" and encouraged him and would later write him a letter that contained some lines from a poem that Yogi treasured for the rest of his life: "There is a destiny that makes us all brothers, none goes his way alone. All that we send into the lives of others comes back into our own."

Without the football scholarship that had paid his way to the University, Yogi could no longer afford to attend school and moved back home. Overcome by humiliation and discouragement, Yogi believed that he had failed at the most important opportunity that God had ever given to him.

Being back at home was difficult, for there were family and friends who had always wondered if maybe Yogi had been a little too "big for his own britches" with his grandiose dreams and ambitious plans. After all, he was just a poor boy from Reeds, North Carolina. What in the world would make him think he was good enough to be a college man, much less a college athlete? Now he was back where he belonged, living with people who had always accepted the path that had been laid before them: a steady job at the mill, a paycheck that was never quite enough, maybe a family and a simple life that should be enough to make anyone reasonably happy.

Yogi worked hard to fight the creeping darkness that hovered about him during those first weeks at home. At the ECU infirmary, the compassion and encouragement from the school nurse had given him enough hope to keep the depression at bay; however, coming home a failure had taken him to the breaking point. With each passing day, he sank deeper and deeper into dark waters of depression. The constant, searing pain of his back injury, the loss of his beloved sports and a future that seemed to mock his years of effort nearly broke him.

As his physical recovery slowly progressed, Yogi's emotional health teetered delicately in the balance. He soon realized that to fully recover he would have to set new goals and fix his eyes upon new mountains to climb. He decided that somehow he had to find his way back to college and the degree he had always dreamed about.

It was then that Yogi took a crucial, courageous step for a boy who had always been so self-sufficient. He sought out the help of a psychologist who could help him face his depression and confront the issues driving it that were now threatening to scuttle all of his dreams.

After a couple of weeks of very hard work, Yogi began to see improvement. Before long, with the encouragement of this counselor, Yogi moved away from home and into a single room set above a drugstore for which he paid $2 a month in rent. He ventured out and found a sales position at a local clothing store where he could earn money for school and living expenses. Soon he was earning enough to pay his own tuition at High Point College, where he attacked his business courses with the same passion and intensity he had once used in his slashing runs and punishing blocks.

Yogi soon discovered he had a real talent for business, specifically in sales. He continued his therapy, and gradually the depression began to fade away as he enthusiastically dove into his business studies. Before too long, Yogi found himself building a loyal customer base at the clothing store. He discovered he had strengths and talents that were every bit as exciting as the athleticism of which he had once been so proud. It was an amazing awakening for Yogi, a wonderful revelation that he promised never to take for granted. This aptitude for business and his innate ability to sell were two incredible gifts that became a lifeline he would use to pull himself up out of the darkness.

Yogi smiled broadly as he finished his story with an insight. He had indeed overcome great odds, but it was the journey, not the destination, that had been the real gift. The act of falling down and rising back up had taught him that while we often believe that we are defined by our circumstances, or by the way the world perceives us, it is instead a question of faith. Are we willing to listen to and be led by a God who knows us intimately and who loves us, and who has great provision for our lives? Are we willing to trust that God is indeed big enough to meet our needs?

As each failure and doubt in Yogi's young life was chipped away, new layers were exposed that finally began to reveal a mature and courageous young man who could honestly say that his greatest achievement and satisfaction was ultimately found in the manner in which he faced the struggle itself. He smiled as he told me, with sincere conviction, that it would be that way for my friend Dani as she battled her cancer. He said that regardless of how things turned out for her, what would ultimately define her life would be her faith, courage and willingness to fight the good fight every single day.

I drove back to my office that afternoon with a renewed sense of hope for Dani and for Yogi as well. And I knew that failure would never look the same to me, for I had just learned that, ultimately, it may be the greatest teacher of all.

YARBOROUGH FAMILY: 1971

ALASKA: 2004

YOGI WITH HIS GRANDDAUGHTER, MAGGIE: 2003

SANTA CLAUS: 1993

FOOTBALL LEAGUE: 2000

CAYMEN ISLANDS: 2002

BERMUDA: 1994

HORSEBACK IN COLORADO: 2000

YOGI'S FAMILY: 1994

HEALTHFUL LIVING RETREAT, VERMONT: 1994

GREENBRIER COUPLE: 1994

FOOTBALL: 1957

WINGATE FOOTBALL: 1960

YOGI'S FAMILY: 1978

WITH THE BOYS: 1984

BERMUDA: 1967

YOGI'S FAMILY: 2013

CHAPTER 7

THE PARADOXICAL NATURE OF JUSTICE

DISCOVERING THAT LIFE IS INHERENTLY UNFAIR AND
LEARNING THAT TRUE HAPPINESS COMES WHEN WE CEASE
TO WORRY ABOUT OURSELVES AND INSTEAD FOCUS ON
THE NEEDS OF OTHERS

"Justice is truth in action."

~ Benjamin Disraeli

During my life, I have witnessed injustices that not only defy rational explanation, but break my heart and leave festering welts upon my soul. These inequities have on many occasions driven me to wrestle with the paradoxical nature of justice and why it seems to be so frequently and blatantly absent in our world. A child goes hungry, a mother is murdered, a young girl is raped, a brilliant mind goes to waste for lack of funds for college tuition, an otherwise healthy baby in Africa dies from simple diarrhea for want of clean water, and so it goes.

The cruel reality is that we do live in a world that is inherently unjust. With this unfortunate truism in mind, I have often asked myself how I can maintain and defend my steadfast belief in a just and compassionate God after observing more than 50 years of seemingly random injustice. After grappling with this question for years, it was only in the last few months of Yogi's life that I finally came to understand the mystery that is justice.

On my way to Southern Roots for my Friday afternoon lunch with Yogi, the warm late summer sun shone brightly through the windshield, and even with the air-conditioning blasting, I could feel the beads of perspiration rising on my face. The ever-present weight of the Carolina humidity hung heavy in the air as I parked and hustled into the restaurant. I was running late from my last morning appointment with a bright African-American young man and his single mother. They had come to see me about funding for a prestigious overseas study program for which he had recently been selected. It was a tremendous honor and a great opportunity for the rising ninth grader, one that would open his eyes to the vast possibilities that lay waiting for him.

As I strode briskly into the beautifully restored building, I could see Yogi and Raymond "cutting up" while watching the latest bevy of wedding party beauties from our regular spot across the dining room. As I approached the table and dropped into the chair, I could feel their attention shift from the girls to scrutinize the disheveled new arrival. Raymond had his own lunch to go to and excused himself, promising to return in an hour.

We exchanged greetings and Yogi, who always seemed to have a sixth sense about my emotions, asked me what had happened. As the waiter delivered my cold glass of sweet tea, I began to recount my earlier meeting with the young man and his mother. Giving him the condensed version, I shared the young man's exceptional grade point average, his standout athleticism in both football and wrestling, and most important, his respectful and sincere manner.

His mother was a truly good woman who was, unfortunately, another sad cliché in the African-American community. A single mom raising two boys on her own while working two jobs, her husband had been abusive until he finally deserted the family, leaving them with bad memories and no financial support.   It was a typically tragic story, one that I seemed to hear almost daily in working with the African-American community.

The meeting for which they had come to me for help was one that would change the young man's life forever because he had the desire and discipline to rise above his current circumstances. I assured Yogi that I planned to find a way to help him go on that trip. This experience and exposure could change his view of the world and become his ticket out of the poverty cycle. It would expose him to new cultures and fresh ideas, which help inner city kids see beyond the confines of their neighborhoods and give them a sense of the opportunities that lay waiting for them.

As always, Yogi listened intently. He quietly chewed his ice and unconsciously played with the control lever on his wheelchair as I continued to go on about this talented young man and his determined mother.

When Yogi was actively listening, gathering data and trying to understand a problem, he always spoke in a very measured and discerning tone. He finally broke his silence and began reviewing the details of the situation: so the boy's mother was a single mom and very much on her own raising a family; the boy was an outstanding student and athlete; their life had been hard, but the trip was a great opportunity. He paused, smiled and then plainly stated that he didn't understand why I was making it so complicated, "For heaven's sake," he said, "I'll pay for the boy to go on his trip."

The problem, I explained, was so much greater than sending this one boy on a trip. Yes, I had no doubt that we could certainly meet this young man's immediate need; however, he represented a seemingly endless line of young, talented African-American boys who were growing up without fathers. He was part of an entire generation who were approaching manhood without a firm, masculine hand guiding them and teaching them right from wrong. To make it even worse, the mother had told me that the most damaging influences were coming from her son's own peers, other African-American boys. His classmates and teammates had been letting him know on a daily basis that publicly displaying intelligence and ambition weren't part of the true persona a young man of color should strive to achieve. Even with all the success he was experiencing in sports and in school, and I'm talking about success that was already making a huge positive impact in his life, he was being pressured to underachieve by those who should have had been his greatest advocates.

When his mother first shared this, I felt an immediate flash of anger surge through me. This outstanding young man seated before me with his head bowed in embarrassment was being ridiculed and ostracized by his own peers for simply trying to reach his fullest potential. Like so many other boys in our community, this young man was fighting the absolutely obscene misconception that young black men pursuing excellence in academics and character were somehow betraying their culture.

Yogi nodded and told me that he completely understood my frustration. Then he asked what my response to the young man had been. I leaned a little closer as I told Yogi how I had risen up from my desk, walked over to the boy, knelt on the floor in front of him, and placed my hands on his strong shoulders and gave him a firm squeeze as I peered intently into his eyes. I then told him that the color of a man's skin has nothing to do with his intelligence, and that anyone who told him so, white or black, was the very worst kind of racist.

I further explained that God had blessed him with remarkable talents and an awesome mother who loved him, believed in him, and who was willing to fight for opportunities that could nurture and grow his talents. Reminding him that these talents were gifts from God that came with great responsibilities and expectations, I then made him promise me that he would never allow anyone to ever stand between him and his dreams. I added, the next time someone gave him a hard time about doing the right things, he should remember that one day in the not too distant future that guy would be washing his BMW. That got a smile out of both mother and son.

Yogi, who had been nodding thoughtfully as I spoke, then told me matter-of-factly that I had done the right thing, but he once again admitted that he still didn't understand why I was so infuriated about it all. He reasoned that if we could help this young man, then surely we could help the others. I shook my head as I explained how many others there were out there just like this young man who did not have a champion, like this amazing mother, to fight for them. I told Yogi that it was almost inevitable that we would lose so many of these young, promising African-American boys to drugs, gangs, crime and violence. It felt like the odds were stacked against these boys and that the chances of them receiving the guidance, love, inspiration and discipline necessary to succeed were almost nonexistent.

How could they be successful in school, qualify for and attend college, and one day find themselves economically and morally viable enough to give back to the next generation of boys in their community? It just seemed inherently unfair to me that this abdication of responsibility by African-American men in the inner cities of America was depriving so many deserving young men of their shot at the "American Dream."

When I finished my tirade, Yogi leaned back in his wheelchair and thoughtfully ran his hands through his hair. He told me in a soft but firm tone that life is rarely fair and that he wasn't so sure it was supposed to be. He reminded me that God was always in control, but this issue was not of his doing; it was ours. God gives us all the choice, "free will," the double-edged sword that allows fathers to choose to either stay or go. They, and they alone, choose to abandon their families, to become involved in criminal activities, drugs, the endless cycles of incarceration, and to pass their sad legacy along to the next generation. Life, Yogi told me, was all about choices, not fairness. Fairness is relative and the reality is that this perceived social injustice is not about fairness as much as it is really an issue of the heart.

From my expression, Yogi could tell I wasn't buying it. Undeterred, he went on. He said that while most fathers want the very best for their children, sometimes, no matter how hard they try, forces beyond their absolute control keep them from being able to provide for their children. Of course, Yogi had a story, and this story, he warned me, was about justice and how it ultimately comes down to a decision of the heart.

Years before, when Yogi's boys were in middle school, his son, Scott, experienced an ill-fated campaign to become president of his seventh grade class. Scott was, and is, a very sincere and earnest redhead who had inherited his father's knack for organization, preparation and business. While he was not the blue chip athlete that his brother, Preston was, he was very capable in nearly any sport he attempted because of his perseverance and desire to serve the greater good. He was a quiet leader who sought justice in all things, who treated everyone, regardless of their station, with honor and respect. Because of this mindset, he assumed everyone else did the same.

Scott's sense of right and wrong, fairness and injustice, was tested that year when he decided to run for class president against a very popular incumbent. Yogi recounted how diligently Scott worked on his campaign materials, how he had crafted, edited and compulsively rewritten his speech, and how he had studied and incorporated the strategies that he used in his very ambitious campaigning to his classmates.

Scott's opponent was a really popular kid, and like most school elections, popularity was a huge factor in the ultimate voting results. However, to everyone's surprise, Scott's persistence and tireless campaigning turned the election into a real horserace. Yogi and Martha could not have been more proud of their son as they watched Scott learning and incorporating many of the leadership characteristics that he would one day use to make himself the successful businessman he would become at Dell Inc. in Austin, Texas.

The day of the election finally arrived. By all indications it was going to be an extremely close race. The two young men were neck and neck until a teacher intervened. Yogi never knew why, or how, but this teacher's intervention destroyed all the hard work, momentum and good intentions of young Scott's campaign. When the votes were counted, the popular incumbent retained his presidency and life went on.

Why this teacher got involved in the outcome of the election is not known. Perhaps she thought the reigning president was the best person for the job; maybe she doubted Scott's ability to carry out his duties; or it could have been that she just didn't like the boy. Whatever the reason, Scott was devastated. After school that day, Scott quietly made his way home to the Yarborough house, barely ate dinner and retired early to his room to try to understand why this teacher had betrayed him.

Like his son, Yogi was stunned by the actions of the teacher, and his immediate reaction was to seek out justice. He considered marching into the headmaster's office and demanding the teacher's head for this blatant violation of trust and fair play.

Yogi paused at this point in the story and shook his head. I heard him chuckle softly and sadly as he surveyed the room for what seemed an eternity before asking me what I thought a father should do at a moment like that. What do you do when your child encounters his first taste of injustice, when a young man's, your young man's vision of a fair and equitable world is shattered?

By this time, Yogi had me on the edge of my seat, waiting breathlessly for the rest of the story. I fully expected a clever and successful resolution that would have put his son into his rightful presidency, but that was not to be.

Yogi told me that he had finished dinner that night and slipped outside to walk around his gardens before going to talk to his son. He had felt that familiar rush as he breathed in the crisp fall air and listened intently to the wind that was whistling through the pine trees bordering his property. He could hear the snorting and pawing of his horses, the soft braying of his midget goats in the pasture, and an occasional bark of a lonely dog off in the distance. One of the family Schnauzers sauntered over and gently nudged Yogi with a moist nose and then stared up at him expectantly, as if to prod him to action. After all, he seemed to say, there was a young boy with a heavy heart sitting alone in his bedroom waiting to hear some wisdom from his father.

Scott was reading when Yogi entered his room, but he could tell the boy had been crying. He sat down on the bed and told Scott that he loved him, how proud he was of him, and that he understood his disappointment. He then told his son about the promising future that lay ahead of him that would, no doubt, include many more injustices. He might one day have a boss who was unfair, a friend who might betray him. He could get unjustly cut from a team or maybe receive a lower grade than he deserved. Life, he told his son, was inherently unfair. Injustice will take place, and it will most certainly happen to him and the ones he loved. He explained that it would be up to him to decide how he would deal with it because fairness is never a given and will always depend on the presence of people with character, integrity and compassion.

Scott intently listened as Yogi leaned over, put his arms around the boy and kissed the top of his head. He told his son what the teacher had done with the election was wrong, and that he could not fathom why an adult would do something like that. He said that he knew his son was a young man of integrity who had worked hard and had deserved to win.

The reality, however, was that he had not won, and it was times like this that every man must seek the depth of his own character. He explained that the manner in which we deal with injustice ultimately reveals the true measure of our own faith and character. Yogi then told his son that they could go to school together the next day, call this teacher on the carpet and demand justice. Or, they could just let it go, forgive the teacher, remember how badly the injustice felt and become a better man for it.

Yogi suddenly grew quiet and I waited for a few seconds before I asked what happened next. He told me that Scott decided that evening to be a man who operated from his values, not his emotions. Yogi said that he knew as he hugged his son that night that Scott would always be a seeker of justice, for he had learned the pain that injustice can bring. This was how he always thought of Scott, Yogi said, as a young man who championed others, who seeks justice and who understands the true meaning of servant leadership.

Just like that, I got it. In that moment, my perspective on the social inequities that had so burdened me as I entered the restaurant that day had changed. I realized now that injustice would always be here. It is the nature of our world. I understood that God was big enough to address injustice and he does so through the hearts of men like Yogi, Scott and, hopefully, me.

I have kept up with that young man who had touched my heart that day in my office. Instead of dwelling on the injustices of his life, I have done my very best to encourage, inspire and be the positive change that every young man deserves to have in his life. You know what? It works.

CHAPTER 8

MENTORING...
THE FOOTPRINTS WE LEAVE BEHIND

COMING TO GRIPS WITH THE REALITY THAT THE ONLY
THINGS WE TRULY LEAVE BEHIND ARE THOSE PARTS OF
OURSELVES WE HAVE ALREADY GIVEN AWAY

*"No greater privilege can come to any person than to stand at the
threshold of the life of a youth with character-kindling power."*

~ John R. Mott

*"It is the nature of man to rise to greatness
if greatness is expected of him."*

~ John Steinbeck

The opening lines of T.S. Eliot's poem, The Wasteland, say that April is the cruelest month. It always made me wonder what terrible misfortunes had befallen this acclaimed poet during a month in which most people are celebrating the arrival of spring. I also find it somehow depressing that of all the wonderful poetry I studied over the course of my education at High Point College, these are the verses I remember with such clarity.

In my own life, it is September, not April that seems to be the harbinger of disaster and strife. During my year of walking alongside Yogi, September was shaping up to be a real benchmark in T. S. Eliot's slightly revised rule of seasonal disasters and in my ongoing education as a father.

My son, Jordie, then 13 years old, had spent his summer playing some of the very best soccer of his young life. In fact, he had been selected for the North Carolina Olympic Development Team and was chosen to take a trip to Alabama for a week of training at the Regional Olympic Development Program Camp under the watchful eyes of the U.S. National Coaching Staff.

Upon his return from camp, I sensed a new air of confidence about him, which seemed like a good thing at the time. However; it would not be long before I found myself rethinking this initial assessment.

I don't know if it was his newly discovered independence, emerging testosterone or simply growing pains, but Jordie's start to the new academic year was proving to be a rocky one.

His school, a local Christian academy, has a highly structured demerit system that is designed to teach boundaries and promote inner discipline. Within the first week of school, however, it was becoming painfully clear that my son was bent on exploring the outer reaches of this system. In return for his efforts, he began to accumulate a staggering number of demerits.

The infractions were innocuous at first: an untucked shirt, a late arrival to class or the inability to keep his mouth shut. The list was soon to become legion.

As the demerits piled up, Jordie would occasionally find himself attending after-school detention. This would serve to quiet things for a day or so, after which time he would resume his march toward another infraction and more detentions. And so the fall semester went.

It soon became clear to all of us that my son was not getting the message, so I set up a meeting with the JV soccer coach and middle school principal, Tim Kohns, a modern-day saint who is absolutely worthy of canonization, to discuss a strategy to address the issue head on. During that meeting, we decided that cutting Jordie's playing time during the middle school's soccer games might get his attention and guide him back to the straight and narrow path. Over the next couple of weeks, however, the demerits continued to accrue, and I watched in horror as his bench time increased from 10 minutes to 15 minutes, then to half an hour, until he was finally sitting out an entire game.

Needless to say, the situation was swiftly spiraling out of control, and I was beginning to panic. Our plan was not curbing his bad behavior at school; it was, in fact, undermining the performance of his soccer team as well as creating tremendous pressure at home. To make matters even worse, Jordie still didn't seem to understand the destructive influence his behavior was having on his classmates, nor did he realize the seriousness of his situation with the school's leadership.

After another couple of weeks, Jordie had become a constant fixture at the afternoon detention sessions, he had been grounded, he had his PlayStation™ impounded and he continued to see his soccer time rapidly dwindling away. Despite all of this, there was still no visible improvement in his behavior or attitude. So once again, he and I went back to revisit the issue with the principal.

This meeting definitely had ominous undertones; we were informed in no uncertain terms that Jordie had reached a new disciplinary threshold. Because of his accumulated detentions, he would be serving a day of ISS, in-school suspension. ISS entailed sitting in a small room, by himself, for an entire school day with only his schoolwork to keep him company. Surely, I thought, a day without his buddies would bore him to tears, and hopefully this period of self-reflection would help him to see the extent of his transgressions and coax him back into his former law-abiding self.

The Day of Atonement arrived, and a seemingly repentant Jordie obediently settled into his punishment. Curious about his progress, I slipped out of the office about halfway through the morning and drove over to the school. As I peeked into his "solitary confinement," I immediately noticed the tell-tale wire of his iPod head phones emerging from his shirt collar. I promptly confiscated the device, which I let him know was now gone until Christmas, and assured him that any further monkey business would be dealt with in a similar fashion.

The afternoon went by much more slowly without the music, but the worst was yet to come. When ISS ended, we met again with Tim Kohns, where we learned that if he earned another ISS, Jordie could face expulsion. The words didn't seem to faze my boy, but it struck terror in my heart, I truly loved his school, and I knew it was good for Jordie, even if he didn't think so at the time. I was desperate to make him understand so he could begin to appreciate his situation.

To my great relief, things actually seemed to improve over the next few days. Jordie appeared to be trying to stay out of trouble, and for the first time that fall, there was hope in the Lessard household. I was scheduled to attend a three-day conference in Seattle near the end of September, but was not at all excited about the prospect of being away from home.

It was on the third day of the conference that I received the call from my wife, Jayne. I still vividly remember the day, as it was my birthday, September 22. Jayne quickly and perfunctorily wished me a happy birthday and immediately began to share the bad news. It seemed that Jordie and one of his buddies had gotten into an altercation in the locker room after school. One shove led to another, and a fist fight ensued. This was not the update I was looking for on the anniversary of my 45th year of life.

Jayne informed me that Jordan and I were to meet with Tim Kohns, the athletic director, and both the varsity and JV soccer coaches the next afternoon. It was in the shadow of impending disaster that I flew back to North Carolina to face the music. However, before I was to face the firing squad, I had an appointment with Yogi for our Friday lunch at Southern Roots.

Lunch on that day had a "Last Supper" feel to it that visibly unnerved me. As I shared with Yogi the details of the most recent developments, a sense of uncontrolled panic rose up within me. The thought of Jordie being kicked out of this school, the kind of wonderful environment in which I had always dreamed he could grow up in, nearly had me paralyzed and Yogi picked up on this very quickly.

The bottom line was that Jordie was immature and appeared to be his own worst enemy. I wondered out loud if this could possibly be one of those teachable moments that I could use to speak truth into my wayward son's life. If so, I had absolutely no idea how to go about doing this. After all, I wanted to teach him right from wrong, to be respectful of others, to honor his teachers, and to be a force for good. I thought I had been doing this.

Most of all I wanted him to be a man of character, one who always told the truth, who accepted the consequences of his actions like a man, and who, when the occasion calls for it, sincerely apologizes with truly repentant heart. But in the face of this impending disaster, the price for those lessons seemed to be growing infinitely more costly by the minute.

When I finally finished, Yogi just sat there silently and thoughtfully for a long moment. He smiled, took one last bite of his lunch and slowly began to speak. He explained that I was being offered the awesome privilege to employ the lost art of mentorship, something he considered to be one of the critically important duties a father is called on to provide for his children. He described it as both a challenge and a gift that, if properly dealt with, can become a great blessing to be passed down for generations to come.

Yogi reminded me that mentoring is not an exact science and that, if the truth be known, he had often failed in this area with his own boys. His redemption, in the end, was that he never quit trying, he never stopped loving them and he always, always, held them accountable for their actions.

His eyes grew misty as he told me what truly good hearts his boys possessed and how proud he was that they had grown into fine men who were godly, honest, compassionate and committed to serving others. But, he added, there were plenty of tears, angst and difficult moments that went into forming those noble hearts. This, he believed, was one of the most important accomplishments a father could achieve, the knowledge that he was leaving behind children who cared for others, who protected the weak and who always sought out justice in an unjust world.

Yogi had faithfully led and later walked beside his boys as they made their way into manhood, and he considered this to be one of the great joys of his life. Again, he paused and grinned at the snapshots of those long ago, dog-eared memories. I could see a sense of contentment settle into his expression, which underscored his knowledge that he had done everything in his power to mold the lives of his sons. I desperately wanted to know his secret, to understand the ingredients of this mysterious alchemy that turned boys into men, especially now as my own son seemed so precariously perched upon what looked to be a very steep ledge.

Every child is different, he explained, each with his own strengths and weaknesses. He said that sometimes the best teaching moments with his boys came during the most difficult and painful times, often when he was least prepared and thoroughly overwhelmed. He believed that

God planned it that way. In fact, he said that God probably planned it like that as His way of helping both parties grow closer to Him.

Yogi then shared a story about his oldest boy, Preston, who had always possessed a beautiful and passionate, but sometimes wild, spirit. Preston had been a remarkably gifted soccer player, a graceful athlete who was blessed with both speed and agility. As Preston grew, it became obvious that his natural talent in soccer could take him far in the game. Over the years, Preston dominated in local Little League and quickly worked his way up the local and state soccer pecking order. Before Yogi knew it, his son was playing for the North Carolina Olympic Development Program team, the highest rung on the ladder for high school players. The boy had acceleration, vision and possessed that "fire in the belly" passion all coaches look for in an athlete.

Yogi closed his eyes as he recalled the vision of his fleet-footed son gliding across the soccer field ... a picture of confidence, agility and daring that still evoked a sense of anticipation and fear in his heart.

However, Preston's thrill-seeking spirit went beyond the soccer field, as he loved to approach all of his life at full speed. Nowhere was this more evident than with his love affair with dirt bikes. The boy's dirt bike was a frightening combination of speed and danger that delivered equal parts exhilaration to Preston and terror to his parents.

Yogi really did fear the bike, and he came to rue the day when he gave in to his son's pleas for his first high-powered racing machine. It was inevitable, Yogi told the boy, that he would hurt himself on the bike, and he reminded his son how much he had at stake with his soccer career.

The driving rain outside Southern Roots splashed across the window glass as Yogi gazed off into the now-flooded courtyard. When he turned back to face me, his expression was one of resignation and pain. It seems that just as Preston had begun hearing from college coaches, there had been an accident, a serious one. The crash put

Preston in the hospital and dramatically changed the direction of his life. The extensive injuries to his legs would significantly alter Preston's speed and agility, the very skills that had made him such a force on the soccer field.

The crisis came and went with the sudden violence and abruptness of a bad dream. After the initial shock had subsided, there followed the inevitable denial, the depression, and ultimately the long, arduous and frustrating hours of rehabilitation. The physical gifts that had made athletics so easy for Preston had been irrevocably snatched away. He would never be the same physically gifted player he was before the accident. Both father and son focused all their energies and powers of optimism into the rehabilitation process and never spoke of what had been lost. During those trying days, Yogi found himself in what would prove to be the most important and life–changing teaching moments of his life with his son.

Yogi could have easily resorted to the temporary comfort and familiarity of anger by verbally striking out at the boy and reminding him of the many times he had warned him about the dangers of the dirt bike. But Yogi was sensitive enough to see and appreciate the depth of the boy's loss and pain. He remembered his own back injury that had taken football away from him so many years before. He remembered that defining season of his life when he had so desperately needed a strong shoulder and a guiding hand, but instead was left in haze of depression to sort out his grief and loss on his own. He had promised in the quiet of his bedroom every night as he finished his prayers that it would be different for his boy.

The brash and casual ignorance of youth had irredeemably changed the boy's life forever and his risky behavior no doubt warranted a strong rebuff. Yet, instead of heeding those base and harsher instincts, Yogi knew it was love that the boy needed most as he learned how to cope with his new reality. Both father and son threw themselves into the rehab process, which they made a team project — they talked strategy, prayed about the future, researched and incorporated any type of medical technology that could give the boy a chance to make his way back onto the soccer field. Yogi was at his son's side every step of the way to encourage him, to be that shoulder to cry on and to remind him that he was not alone.

Back in the din of the Friday Southern Roots lunch crowd, Yogi spoke in a voice heavy with emotion as he shared how he had told Preston that he understood the void that accompanies a great loss as well as the sharp pain of remembering what once had been. The lesson to learn, he told him, was that life can be harsh, that bad things do happen to good people and that ultimately anything can be taken away. He assured the boy, however, that the truest measure of a man is the courage and faith with which he confronts his greatest disappointments.

Preston had always possessed a lion's heart and a willing spirit. In time and with a lot of prayer and plenty of hard work, he slowly recovered from his injuries and finally made it back to the soccer field. While his speed and agility never quite returned to its former brilliance, the young man who had suffered through that violent, life-shattering accident would find himself four years later standing with his team in the middle of the Davidson College soccer stadium preparing to play in the NCAA Division 1 men's soccer championship match. On the sidelines stood a proud father with an irrepressible smile who had so many years before found the courage to fight back the fears and disappointments in his own heart so that he could be strong enough to love his son and help guide him back into the game he loved so much.

This kind of mentoring, Yogi said, is the most significant, for it demands that the giver must die to self, suppress the natural inclinations toward disappointment, anger and fear, and simply seek the best for the one he loves. It is an act of complete unselfishness that shifts focus from self interest to the purest and most noble kind of love, a love that enables a son to discover the true greatness that lies within.

Yogi, now exhausted, whispered to me, but mostly I think he was speaking to himself, that seeing Preston out on the field that day with his team sharing in the biggest moment in Davidson College soccer history was one of the happiest moments of his life. He looked up to me with misty eyes and a beaming smile that seemed to light up the entire dining room, and he assured me it was one of those defining father and son moments he will never forget.

As I began settling the bill, I could see Raymond sauntering back into the dining room, and I realized our time was coming to a close. The quiet and engulfing intimacy that Yogi and I had just shared quickly vanished as the room was once again filled with laughter and conversation. Raymond greeted us with his usual playful banter, and as the pair wheeled their way toward the door, Yogi turned back with his trademark grin and reminded me one final time to just love the "little knucklehead."

As I watched them leave, I could feel a profound and encouraging sense of hope in my heart that lightened my step. I resolved to do as Yogi had done with Preston — accept the consequences, no matter how dire they appeared at first, and work with my son to help him learn from his mistakes. This process would no doubt come at a great cost to me personally, but I was now confident in the knowledge that it would one day change his life for the better.

When Jordie and I arrived for the meeting, the group had already decided their course of action. They did not feel that kicking Jordie off the team was in the best interests of the boy or the school. Instead, they would teach him how to become a servant leader. For the next two weeks, Jordie was to serve as the team's manager while his teammates played the three most important games of the season without him. I was overwhelmed by their grace, and I thanked them for their willingness to invest in my son. I told them I was going to add my own little twist to their very generous proposition, which I hoped would further drive home this message of servant leadership.

The games came and went, and to this day I don't remember whether we won or lost. I do, however, keenly remember how it ripped my heart out to watch my son serving out his sentence on the sidelines. But I was so proud of his willingness to serve, to give back to his teammates, and I saw, for the first time, a genuine sorrow for letting them down.

Jordan and I spent the next three weeks following through on my addition to his rehabilitation program by getting up at 5:30 every morning so that he could serve breakfast to the men at the local homeless shelter. Most of these men were lost, discouraged, forgotten and were suffering greatly because of their bad choices. I accompanied him every day and watched as my son learned what it was like to put the needs of others before his own.

He soon discovered the strength and honor that comes from serving others, and he experienced the incredible power that is generated by the simple act of giving at a cost to one's self. He began to grow over those weeks into a young man who would one day compete for a U.S. Academy National Championship, who would become the first recruit signed for 2010 to play soccer at Wheaton College, one of the premier soccer programs in the country, and who would become a mentor and role model at Wesleyan Academy where he would serve as the captain of the very team he had let down a few years earlier.

Jordie never had another serious behavior problem after that eighth-grade year. My dying friend Yogi had once again passed along to me a gift of enduring value, the privilege of mentoring, which enabled me to show my son the character-kindling power that lies within the heart of a godly man.

CHAPTER 9

UNDERSTANDING AND EMBRACING FEAR

LEARNING THAT CONQUERING FEAR IS THE BEGINNING OF WISDOM

"Every man knows the tyranny of fear; the truly courageous ones are those who continue to do the right thing even when they are most afraid."

~ Col. Paul F. Lessard, USMC (ret.)

Fear has been called the great equalizer. It can make a man search deep within himself to find something to sustain him in those moments of desperation and terrifying accountability. Those who were fortunate enough to be loved and mentored well are so much more prepared for these situations because someone — a father, a big brother, a coach or even an older buddy — has spoken the truth about fear. This truth declares that we are all fearful, that fear spares no one, and that only through our understanding and management of fear are we ultimately defined as men and women of faith.

I know something about fear. My moment of truth, or as Teddy Roosevelt once called it, "my crowded hour," happened more than 20 years ago. The anniversary of the event is April 26, and each year I commemorate it the same way, I take flowers to my friend Ella Mae and together we celebrate it as the day we rescued one another.

That day's adventure began just before 5:30 a.m., amidst darkness and a storm in the sleepy Oak Hollow area of High Point. It was Friday, and I was on my way to play an early morning game of squash with a friend in Greensboro. My route that morning was not my normal one, as my wife and I were renting our house out to some folks from California who were in town for the International Home Furnishings Market. This is a common practice in our city of more than 100,000, as Market draws upward of 75,000 people to High Point twice a year. With my wife's parents living just 25 miles away in Winston-Salem, we regularly rented out our home during Market and I commuted to work.

Not being coffee drinkers ourselves, we had not anticipated that our house guests may need a morning jolt of caffeine. So instead of going straight to my squash game, I was driving back to our house located on the far side of Oak Hollow Lake to deliver a borrowed coffee pot to our Market guests.

Halfway to High Point, I realized that I was running late, despite the fact that I had risen at 4:30 a.m. An unusually hard rain was hammering my car, rendering the windshield wipers almost useless.

I would find out later this torrential rain had been falling with this same ferocity throughout the night.

As I reached the outskirts of High Point, I could plainly see I had not allotted myself enough time, and I could feel a sense of panic begin to rise within me. My squash partner that morning was my former boss, mentor and friend, Phil Watson, a Harvard MBA, who valued punctuality above all else.

When I finally turned on to Main Street, I suddenly remembered a shortcut to the lake. A few weeks prior, I had run in a 5k road race that had taken me through the back streets of west High Point. The city watershed, Oak Hollow Lake, was located there, and the shortcut I had discovered would take me around the lake and save me a good 10 minutes.

As I hurdled up the gradual incline of leafy Shadybrook Drive, it was still pitch black and the pummeling of the rain upon my windshield seemed to have actually intensified. The street crested, and then dropped dramatically toward the lake area. It was only at the very last second that I managed to hit the brakes in time to keep myself from plunging into the flooded street before me. The night-long deluge of rain had caused the lake and its feeder creek to swell well beyond its banks and over into the street. There was more than five feet of water surging violently down the road, taking everything in its path through the normally placid creek bed.

My initial reaction was one of relief that I caught myself in time, and then once again panic set in as I remembered the squash game and realized I was now even later than before. Anxious to make up for lost time, I put the car in reverse and began to hurriedly back away when I thought I caught the briefest glimpse of a white object that seemed to be swirling and bobbing in the surging waters before me.

After lowering my window and peering out into the rain, I could just make out a man wearing a white T-shirt who appeared to be riding on top of a large Oldsmobile station wagon that was bobbing violently and sinking fast into the swirling rapids. Much later we would learn that the car was going down into more than twenty feet of dark, muddy water.

I was out of my car at this point yelling to the figure in white and trying hard to make out his words as he yelled frantically above the rain and the wind. As I moved forward, walking into the water, I thought I heard him say that an elderly woman was trapped in the car. The man, Jack Kavanough, who had risen early that morning to run, had seen the rain and decided to head back to bed when he saw the woman unknowingly drive into the water. In a matter of seconds, the car had slid off the bridge, drifted into the current and was very quickly pulled out into the surging waters. He had been unsuccessful in his attempts to get her out of the car, as the electric locks and windows would not work and now he needed me to get help ... fast!

Of course, this incident took place before all of us carried cell phones. It was immediately evident to me that I did not have time to find a phone, make a call and wait around for the police to arrive. We needed to get that poor woman out of the car before it disappeared under the rapidly rising waters. Knowing I was going to end up in the water eventually, I stripped off my squash clothes down to my compression shorts, to minimize the extra weight of wet clothing. Then it suddenly struck me that I had nothing with which to pry, cut or hammer my way into the car. I quickly surveyed the surrounding area and located the nearest house. As I ran through the rain dressed only in my shorts, I was praying that the folks in that house didn't scare easily and had access to some tools.

I have always believed in divine intervention and never was it more evident than that morning in the driving rain. There I was, thoroughly soaked and nearly naked, pounding on the door when a startled young woman opened it and actually let me in! I would later learn that she and the others staying in the home worked for the same company as Jack (the man on the Oldsmobile station wagon) and had rented the place for the duration of the Furniture Market.

Picture this scene in your mind: a young out-of-towner is awakened from a deep sleep by an unshaven man with wild hair and who is wearing only what appeared to be really tight, now see-through underwear. And it's only 5:15 in the morning. I doubt too many people would have opened their door that morning to talk to, much less help, an apparent lunatic, but this young woman did. Upon hearing the urgent nature of my mission, she immediately directed me to a tool room where I retrieved a small hammer and a huge plumber's wrench that would nearly drown me minutes later during my desperate swim to the car.

After yelling back to my new friend to call 911, I sprinted across the large front yard and dove into the dark churning waters. The car was nearly submerged now and I am not ashamed to say that I was terrified as I struggled to catch my breath. I have always been a strong swimmer, having grown up in the Philippine Islands where I had learned to swim with my mother in the South China Sea. But that morning, the current I was fighting was much stronger than it had looked.

With a hammer in one hand and a plumber's wrench in the other, I felt myself being rapidly pulled back toward the viaduct that flowed under the road and into the lake where I kept envisioning they would discover all three of us days later.

After three attempts, I finally reached the car, which was now submerged up to the back window. Jack had moved off the roof and onto the back bumper of the car, and when I was close enough, he pulled me up from the water. From our perch on the back bumper, we could see that the interior of the station wagon was completely flooded and the elderly woman was floating limp and unconscious right before our eyes in the murky water.

The next few minutes were a blur. I called out to Jack to cover his eyes as I smashed the rear window with the hammer. In an instant, the car disappeared beneath the waves and we both lunged into the car reaching for the woman. I managed to grab her leg, while Jack had hold of her arm. For what seemed like an eternity, we struggled to get her out of the car as it continued to sink. While we both feared that our efforts might be in vain, neither of us was willing to let go of her. We knew that once we let go, we would never be able to find this poor woman in the dark and muddy flood waters.

Only God knows how we managed to pull her out of the car, but we suddenly found ourselves gasping for air at the surface. When we got our bearings, we realized that the three of us were pinwheeling toward the viaduct. With both of us still straining to maintain our tenuous grip on the woman's limp, unconscious body, Jack somehow managed to reach out and grab a branch from an overhanging tree. As it turns out, Jack saved all of our lives by making that last-minute grab. The momentary respite allowed me to change my grip and grab the woman under her arm, which in turn gave us the leverage to begin fighting our way out of the current.

God was certainly in the water with us that morning. When we finally reached the shore, we were cold, exhausted and frantic to see the condition of this woman we had refused to leave behind. Somehow in the process of pulling her body out of the water one of us must have accidentally performed a Heimlich maneuver, which caused her to suddenly and violently regurgitate an unbelievable amount of lake water. Above the roar of the water all we could hear was this wonderful sound of this old country girl screaming at the top of her lungs, "Help me, Jesus! Help me, Jesus!"

At this point, Jack and I were elated that we had not only survived the rescue, but also appeared to have revived our new friend. In the midst of our relief, the woman, whose named we learned was Ella Mae, turned to me and rasped that she thought she was having a heart attack! We quickly carried her to the house where I had retrieved the tools earlier. I very quickly exhausted all of my first aid training when to the relief of all, the EMTs arrived. They took over, as Jack and I both stepped away and began to shake. After a brief exam, one of the EMTs turned to us with a big grin on this face and told us that Ella Mae was going to be fine. It seemed that the pressure she was experiencing in her chest was due to the large amount of water she had ingested when she had drowned. She was definitely uncomfortable, but she was not having a heart attack and looked like she would recover completely.

Jack and I, drenched to the bone and freezing, were both covered in blood. After a few moments of frantic searching, we found that the only injury to either of us was a small cut I had received on my right hand that was bleeding like crazy. As the EMTs wheeled Ella Mae out to the ambulance, I suddenly remembered that my squash partner, my former boss, the Harvard MBA who hated having to wait, was standing all by himself in the empty squash court thinking he'd been stood up!

As I look back, I can say that two things enabled me to rise above my fear and complete the mission that morning. The first was the constant refrain of my daughter's favorite Bible song that had been coursing through my brain reminding me that "I can do all things through Christ who strengthens me." The second was a conversation I had shared with my father nearly thirty years before.

It was 1968, and my father had just returned from Vietnam. We were going through his locker box one morning when I asked him, in the random way children do, if he had ever been afraid in the war. It would have been easy for him to have taken the standard Marine Corps approach and tell me that "fear is weakness" and it had no place in the heart of a real man. Instead, he looked directly into my eyes and told me he had never been so afraid in all his life. He said that anyone who says differently is either a liar or crazy. He went on to explain that all of us experience fear at some point in our lives, and it doesn't make you any less of a man. He said he always prayed that God would give him the strength to do his duty, even when he was most afraid. This, he said unashamedly, had happened several times during his tour in Vietnam and he was grateful that despite the overwhelming fear he had always done his duty, with God's help.

My father's words had saved me on that rainy morning at the lake.

They gave me the freedom to be human, to feel the fear and still carry on. Most of all, they enabled me to look beyond myself and rely on a power so much greater than my own.

Ella Mae survived her ordeal and over the years became my dear friend and second mother who called me regularly to make sure I was eating my vegetables and getting enough sleep. Jack and I have remained friends over the years, and almost one year after the rescue we were awarded the Carnegie Hero Medals, our nation's highest civilian recognition for bravery. In 1996, we had the privilege of running together with the Olympic Torch during the Torch Run for the Atlanta Olympics, and Ella Mae was there to hug us both as we passed along the Eternal Flame.

As I wheeled Yogi into the Southern Roots dining room that day, I was thinking about Ella Mae. I had visited her a couple of weeks earlier, which always reminded me of the fear I had experienced during that early morning miracle. On this day, I could not help but wonder what my friend Yogi might have to say about fear.

The conversation that followed was as illuminating and reassuring as the talk I had shared with the Colonel so many years before, for it dealt with a different and even more devastating form of fear … fear of the inevitable.

Yogi's physical condition was deteriorating more rapidly now, as his illness had spread to both legs. It was beginning to affect his arms, as well. Most discouraging of all, it was moving into his chest, which made his breathing more difficult.

Respiratory failure is one of the most common causes of death for ALS patients, and that afternoon I could hear a slight wheezing as Yogi worked his way through his meatloaf.

Yogi responded to my question about fear with a smile as he began sharing with me his lifelong acquaintance with fear. He began by explaining that there are several kinds of fear and that the worst of these is not life threatening.

He began recounting his experiences with poverty, failure and depression, experiences that he believed were much more devastating than cancer or ALS. These were stifling fears that are painfully imbedded in a person's very soul, and they are leering reminders of an inadequacy that peers into your heart 24 hours a day. He said he would take cancer over those demons any day of the week. He further explained that immediate and urgent fear is always easier to manage and, while not meaning to offend me, he noted that my rescue incident, while heroic, took less than eight minutes. Imagine, he said, living with that same intensity of fear for days on end. He went on to share how brutal this unrelenting fear can be — an eroding presence that not only wears down confidence, but it ultimately destroys all sense of hope.

It was obvious that Yogi had experienced this dehumanizing fear in his life, so I asked him to tell me when it was that he was most afraid. His answer caught me by surprise, it had been the Repo man! Really, he assured me, he was not kidding! Yogi shook his head as he remembered a time when he feared, on a daily basis, that the bank might come and take away the cars he had given to his boys when they were in high school.

It had happened in the late '80s after an unforeseen business reversal. The trouble began with a betrayal. People in whom Yogi had put his trust had left his business and taken key clients with them. Sales, revenues and cash flow were immediately and dramatically impacted.

Over the years, Yogi has always been generous to a fault. His accountant once told me that at times he ran his company like it was an extension of the Salvation Army. That's why this betrayal devastated Yogi so completely, for he took great pride in the fact that his company provided for the livelihood of hundreds of people. Now, through no direct fault of his own, he was suddenly facing a business challenge that appeared to be more than his talent and assets could overcome. Most devastating was that he was not only letting down his employees who had always counted on him, but his own family as well.

Just as in every challenge he had ever faced, Yogi did what had to be done. He met with his bankers, he talked with his financial people, and they all told him the same thing. It was time to shut the operation down. The damage had been done and the logical thing to do, in their opinions, was to close the business.

It was during this time of confusion and upheaval that Yogi learned a valuable lesson; the only way a man can face such overwhelming fear and not let it defeat him is by completely relying on his faith, character and prayer. There's a verse in the book of Hebrews that exhorts believers to walk by faith, not by sight, and it was this that Yogi carried with him as he struggled to reach a decision.

The easy way out was to shut the company down, to let go of the loyal employees who had worked with him for so many years and simply to take what he had tucked away for his family and move on. But how could he let these people down? If he allowed this to happen, how could he ever look at himself in the mirror again? And what message would it send to his sons?

It was not the issue of losing the money that troubled Yogi so much; he reasoned that he had lived through hard times and he was confident that even if he lost everything, he had the ability to earn it all back. However, it was the idea of failing those people he had come to love as family that stopped Yogi from following his advisors' counsel. After all, he had watched these men and women become proud and capable employees. He had seen them raise their own families, build their own homes and send their children to college. He believed they deserved to live and retire in dignity.

Yogi's stare pierced me as he explained how the gut-wrenching fear of making a decision that could impact the lives of your family for years to come can eat at your soul every day. He vividly recalled fear's bitter tasting bile being with him in the morning, as he worked through the day and when he lay awake in his bed trying in vain to sleep.

Yogi was then and always would be committed to loving and respecting others, and the decision he made one afternoon alone in his office spoke more about courage than almost anything I had ever heard before or since. His CFO and dear friend, Dale Singly, had laid out all the numbers, and no matter how he tweaked them, the answer remained the same — the business simply could not go forward without a significant infusion of capital. Yogi already knew this and he smiled as he reiterated for what was probably the thousandth time that he simply could not let all these people go.

The next day, he called Dale into his office and told him that he and Martha had decided to put their own retirement money back into the company. It was the least they could do, he told Dale, for all those folks who had helped him build this company.

Dale and all the other financial advisors begged Yogi to reconsider. They assured him that businesses go under all the time and that there was nothing dishonorable about moving on. They reminded him that he had already provided years of leadership, support, wages and benefits to the employees of his company.

Yogi's response was brief and to the point. He said that his greatest fear was that his heart and faith were not strong enough to do what was right in the eyes of God. This was the worst fear imaginable, a fear that he never wanted to confront again after that day.

Yogi had faced many demons in his life, but nothing had shaken him like that battle. The retirement money was invested into the company, and for more than 18 months, Yogi drew no salary. Times were tight; Yogi fretted over how the sacrifices were impacting his wife and kids, but it was no longer the agonizing fear that had tested his soul. In fact, Yogi would say with complete confidence later on that the 18 months they spent working to save his company were the most fulfilling of his business career. He believed that his boys heard the message loud and clear, we can never let fears dictate our ability to do that which is right.

Yogi's company gradually became profitable again, and within four years it was stronger than ever. More important, Yogi was stronger and grateful for what he felt was the most defining season of his life.

Back in the Southern Roots dining room, Yogi reveled in the sweet memory of that long ago victory. It was like watching an old athlete remembering past glories with the intimate acknowledgement of the sacrifices made and the hard-won victory they ultimately produced. He turned to me and softly told me that he was saddened at the thought of dying, but he was not afraid. While he was leaving behind those he loved most, he had never once feared his impeding death because he had slain much bigger demons in his lifetime and he had the scars to prove it.

As I settled the bill and we prepared to leave, I felt a wave of love and admiration for my friend wash over me. I believed him when he said he was not afraid to die. I could see in my friend's amazing courage that once we really conquer fear, we gain an inner strength that can carry us through anything.

This knowledge and the sense of peace it brings allows us to pass this blessing on to those we love; after all, there is no better legacy we can leave behind than the gift of courage.

CHAPTER 10

THE COURAGE TO FINISH STRONG

TO KNOW THAT AT THE END OF ONE'S LIFE, IT IS
THE FAITH, COURAGE AND COMPASSION WE HAVE
DISPLAYED AND THE LIVES WE HAVE TOUCHED THAT
WILL DETERMINE OUR TRUE LEGACY

"I have fought the good fight, I have finished the race.

I have kept the faith."

~ 2 Timothy 4:7

It was December 2005, and I was working late at the Foundation office when the call came from Martha. Yogi had just been rushed to the hospital in severe respiratory distress. I could tell by Martha's tone it was bad. For several weeks, he had been experiencing more and more trouble breathing, and that evening at his home the situation had suddenly become critical. As I drove across town to the High Point Regional Health System, I caught myself reflecting upon the cruel and unpredictable nature of this disease that seemed to take a slightly different tack with each life it invaded.

Some patients experienced a sudden and overwhelming assault that takes its course in a swift and deadly manner. Others, like Yogi, experience incremental episodes that gradually render different parts of the body useless. For Yogi it had begun in his right leg, moved to his left leg and it wasn't long before he began to feel the weakness moving into his arms. By late November, it was beginning to affect his breathing. The doctors said that once the respiratory stage of the disease began, it typically meant that the end was near. Even though I knew intellectually it was coming, the thought of this impending disaster seemed to engulf me and totally unnerved me.

I was not prepared for the scene I encountered when I entered Yogi's hospital room that evening. He was lying on his side teetering on the edge of the bed, desperately struggling for each breath. There was a look of absolute terror and exhaustion in his eyes that reached right into my chest and gripped my heart. Nurses were working frantically, and the alarms of various pieces of medical monitoring equipment were filling the air with the sounds of technology gone mad. Martha was in tears, and the moment my eyes met Yogi's, I knew that this was indeed the beginning of the end. Yet, in the midst of all the noise and confusion, Yogi reached out and pulled me close as he gasped his now familiar refrain that even then, even in the terror of that moment, God was still good. I managed a weak smile and gripped his hand tighter.

On several occasions recently, I caught myself praying that God would be merciful in the way in which he took Yogi "Home," and this terrifying scene was not what I had envisioned. The sensation of not being able to breathe creates a very intense feeling of panic, a terrible physical discomfort and an unremitting fatigue that feels like it is slowly pulling you under. I had experienced this sensation once in my life — a soccer injury in which I broke several ribs and collapsed a lung — so I knew all too well what my friend was going through. It is unlike any other sensation I've ever experienced, like drowning on dry land, and it creates a lasting memory of desperation and trauma that remains with you for the rest of your life.

As I stood beside Yogi's bed and continued to hold his hand, I could feel his body and his spirit fighting courageously in unison. Watching him violently gasping for air, then spasm and shudder and then desperately repeat the process again, I could not help but wonder how long he could sustain this Herculean struggle. After what seemed like an eternity, the medication finally began to kick in, and I watched my friend's body begin to relax into a more normal breathing rhythm. Within a few minutes, he was asleep as the rest of us shell-shocked survivors looked on in a state of silent and utter disbelief.

As Martha walked me to the elevator, I could plainly see that the trauma and emotion of the past year's unrelenting battles were taking their toll. Martha had always possessed a youthful, natural beauty that, when combined with her upbeat and dynamic personality, made her appear decades younger than her actual age. However, that night I could not help but notice the fatigue and worry etched upon her pretty face. Before I stepped into the elevator, I embraced her tightly as I softly implored her to try to get some rest. No other words were spoken, and in the silence, we held each other tightly as our shared discouragement and exhaustion eddied and pooled between us.

Within a few days, Yogi was released from the hospital and life gradually regained the subdued rhythms of a crisis temporarily forestalled. The terror of the episode was quickly tucked away and forgotten, never discussed, as if ignoring it might somehow make it go away.

Yogi and I continued to meet for our lunches, and I fine-tuned his eulogy with a new sense of urgency. It was during one of these discussions that he taught me his final and most elegant lesson of all — how to die with grace and dignity.

My friend was never quite the same after that episode in the hospital, for his strength and endurance had irrevocably diminished. Our Friday talks moved from our beloved vantage point in the Southern Roots dining room to Yogi's home, where we would meet in the den, which we shared with his ever vigilant Schnauzers and his dreamy-eyed Golden Retriever. Our lunches were now much shorter in duration, and they would always end with Yogi valiantly, but unsuccessfully, fighting to stay awake.

One particular afternoon, I began our session by simply asking how he was preparing for what lay ahead. Yogi flashed a wry smile and chuckled as he reminded me that we're all going to die one day. The only difference between us, he told me, was that his time was coming sooner rather than later.

He assured me that God had given him a fuller and more complete life than any he could have imagined and he had no regrets. He told me that he and Martha truly loved one another and that they had been a team committed to each other through thick and thin. His relationships with his sons had always been a daily reminder of God's faithfulness, as they had been unexpected gifts from a compassionate and loving God. He believed he had passed on everything he knew to help his boys become the men they were created to be. He choked back the tears as he whispered, almost to himself, that in their finest moments together their "souls had met." What more, he asked, could a father ask for?

Yogi's single greatest regret, he said, was that he wouldn't live to see his grandchildren grow up. He made me promise the book I would later write about his life would convey to Nathan and Maggie the depth of his love for them and explain to them how difficult it was for him to leave them. He adored his grandchildren; being with them had brought him unimaginable joy and fulfillment. Most of all, he wanted them both to know that his spirit and his love would be with them always, to look after them and protect them for the rest of their lives.

Yogi wiped his eyes and smiled. He then whispered, as if in prayer, that the people he had known and loved – his family, friends, employees and running buddies – were what he would miss most.

In that moment of quiet reflection, I could see that he was beginning to make his final spiritual and emotional preparations, so I asked Yogi to tell me where he felt God had been throughout these most difficult months of his struggle. Almost instantaneously his demeanor changed and his response was resolute as he asked me to remember back, early in our journey. He reminded me of the day when he had told me that he would never, ever, ask "why," that he would never feel sorry for himself and that he would never waste a moment in regret.

Yogi was still convinced that everything had happened for a reason, more specifically, it had happened for a divine purpose. He believed that God had used his illness to reach out to the hundreds of people who had prayed for him, served him and his family, and who had witnessed both the triumphs as well as the disappointments. He hoped they had seen a man of faith, someone who did not fear his earthly death, who had persevered with courage and dignity, and who had showed them that through it all, God was always faithful and, yes, always good.

He still thought it was amazing how an illness like ALS could so completely eliminate all the unnecessary distractions in life. The pressures of work, the volatility of the stock market and the hundreds of meaningless preoccupations that had once seemed so important were now so totally inconsequential. He said that his world had grown infinitely smaller as God had taken away his mobility, his independence, his ego and his pride. Yogi found that they had been replaced with a sense of peace and an amazing dependency upon God that he wished he had known before he had taken ill.

God's provision had become so beautifully simple. Through this, Yogi finally understood the depth of His unrelenting love for him. He also saw how wonderfully absurd it was that the God of the universe, the Alpha and the Omega, longed to be in a relationship with him. He said that while it might sound crazy, there were days when he felt almost overwhelmed with joy by God's grace and presence, something he had always been too busy to appreciate.

As his world continued to shrink, it had become increasingly clear to Yogi that there were only three things that really mattered in this world: faith, family and friends. He reasoned that if it had taken ALS to reveal this to him, then it was worth it.

Yogi paused to catch his breath, and I could see that he was tiring, so we decided to wrap it up for the day. He was like a weary old soldier after a long forced march, proud of the ground he had covered and yet so physically and emotionally spent. But before surrendering to his fatigue, he once again took my hand and said in a strong and resolute voice that his greatest desire through it all had been to "run a good race." More than anything, he wanted to finish well.

We sat together for a moment, holding each other's hands, and as I hugged him for what would be the final time, I told him I loved him and was proud of him. I assured him that he was, indeed, finishing well. Then I leaned in close and whispered that being his friend and walking with him these past months was a gift I would always treasure. He gave me a final squeeze of his hand and asked me to always look after Martha and the boys to which I nodded and smiled as I whispered, "I promise."

Before I reached the door, Yogi was asleep. I took one final glance at my slumbering friend, and a familiar verse that we both loved from the book of Hebrews came into my mind: "Faith is the substance of things hoped for and the evidence of things not seen." Perhaps this was what it had all been about: a good man's final walk of faith … a spiritual journey that had touched my life and so many others in a deeply personal and profound way. This was Yogi's ultimate gift to us all.

That was the last time I saw my friend alive. When the phone rang the next afternoon, it was Martha saying that Yogi had been very quiet and sleepy that morning, and had settled down early for a nap. He had simply closed his eyes and passed peacefully away into eternity.

I could feel my heart catch as I realized that my prayers had been answered; my friend had not suffered. As I hung up the phone and gazed out my eighth-story window to see a midwinter dusk descending on the lonely buildings of North Main Street, I silently thanked God for this final act of compassion and mercy.

When I arrived at the Yarborough home that evening, it was surrounded with the cars of friends and family who had gathered to pay their respects to a man who had so permanently altered the way in which all of us would look at life, faith, love and happiness. I sat alone in my car for several minutes trying to take it all in, to come to grips with the reality that Yogi was really gone. I knew that my world, our world, would never be the same and that it was going to be a colder and more colorless world without him.

I found myself retracing the steps of our journey over the last 16 months, the many unforgettable meals we shared at our beloved Southern Roots, the great conversations, the mentoring and the friendship that still felt so intimate and real. With all that had taken place in my life over these past months, Yogi's wisdom, humor and common sense had helped me become a better man, a stronger father and a more committed husband.

At that moment, I realized that Yogi's gift to me had indeed been the privilege of sharing his incredible final journey home. While preparing for what Mrs. Powers once called "her trip across the Jordan," Yogi had allowed me to share in his final walk, to see and feel what most people never experience until their own final days.

He taught me the simple dignity of grace, the nobility of suffering well and the sustaining, all-consuming power of faith. These virtues had enabled him to run the race, to finish well and to bear witness to all that, even in the worst of times, God is with us and that despite the circumstances, He is always good.

I smiled as I considered the magnitude of this gift. Then I laughed out loud in the stillness of my car as I realized that my friend Yogi was even then teaching his final lesson to me from beyond the grave. I shook my head slowly and smiled, as I knew how much he would have enjoyed the idea of this final achievement.

The tears began as I whispered a final farewell to Yogi in my dark and empty car. "Godspeed, my friend; I will see you again. Until then, I will remember you, and I will always remember the true measure of your heart."

EPILOGUE

It is now March 2007. The weather is slowly beginning to warm, giving our town just the slightest hint of the flowers and vegetation that will soon repopulate the gray winter landscape.

It has been a little more than a year since my friend Yogi died, and while his memory is still fresh in my mind and heart, there remains a profound sense of loss that I just can't seem to shake.

Three days after Yogi slipped so peacefully from this world, I delivered his eulogy to a crowd of more than 1,000 of his friends and family at Providence Place where the First Wesleyan Church had so generously offered the use of their amphitheatre. This beautiful structure was one of few local venues large enough to accommodate Yogi's large and diverse collection of friends and family.

The service was unlike any I had ever seen. It was attended by people from every cultural, social, religious, age and economic population in our community and beyond. It was truly a celebration, just as Yogi would have wanted it to be.

As I stood at the podium, I remember feeling Yogi's presence in a very real and tangible way, and it brought a smile to my face. I was surrounded by those people whom Yogi had faithfully loved and who, in turn, had returned his affection and commitment so completely. This amazing picture of love only confirmed to me his often repeated belief that what matters most in life are the relationships.

As I began to deliver my final remembrances of Yogi that night, I looked out over the audience and was awed by the impact this one man had upon so many people. I could see the results of Yogi's compassion and faithfulness etched upon the faces of the countless people he had helped and loved over the years. I saw Yogi's beautiful wife, Martha; his sons, Preston and Scott; his daughter-in-law, Mindy; and his grandchildren, Nathan and Maggie. Just before I began, I whispered a silent prayer that my words that night would communicate the depth and breadth of the love Yogi had for each of them.

As I began to speak of Yogi's life, I could see heads nodding, smiles forming, tears falling and, at times, a chuckle or two, as we all remembered this little man who had such a big heart and who had loved and lived with such utter abandon and joy. I have always believed it is up to us, the living, to bear witness to the lives of those whom we have loved. Those words that I spoke that evening were in many respects a prayer of thanks and, most of all, a love song for a very special friend whose life had really mattered.

After the service concluded, the strangest thing happened — no one left. It appeared that no one wanted to leave and risk losing the feeling of shared intimacy that had settled upon Yogi's very diverse collection of friends. What they did, instead, was to gather in small groups in which they began to share their favorite stories about Yogi. These conversations included touching and hilarious recollections of how this amazing man who had loved to pass out his Tootsie Pops had touched so many lives with his compassion, generosity and love.

In the months that followed, Martha and her family slowly began the painful process of adjusting to the loss of a husband, father, grandfather and friend. There was a palpable void in the hearts of so many in our community, yet there was also a sense of spiritual reassurance and a renewal of faith. We had all witnessed the courage and grace that Yogi had displayed in his final months, and we knew that this strength could only have come from a loving and compassionate God. Yogi had been right after all: Even in the worst of times, God is good.

Yogi had left us a remarkable legacy that continues even now. He taught us that there is nothing so powerful in this life as the example of a man who stays true to his faith and character even as he walks into the shadow of the valley of death.

Was Yogi perfect? Of course, he wasn't. He stumbled and fell just like the rest of us, but we all recognized and admired his resilience, his willingness to pick himself up and carry on even in the midst of great adversity and struggle. He was a man who was always willing to grapple with life, who never gave up, and who ultimately understood that the real glory was "in the struggle." In the end, I could plainly see that Yogi had become so much like his favorite biblical hero, David, who had also experienced so many overwhelming challenges in his life, yet always remained "a man after God's own heart."

So what had I learned in this past year and a half journey spent with my dying friend, Yogi? As I found myself facing the approach of my 50th year of life, I realized he taught me we were created for three simple, yet profound reasons: to be in a love relationship with our Creator, to honor Him in all that we do and say, and to know that in all things, both the good and the bad, God is there and He is always good. Yogi taught me this.

I pray that this book will be an enduring witness of a life well lived and a grateful remembrance of a remarkable friendship. I am privileged to acknowledge and praise his struggle. I love and embrace both the sinner and the saint. I honor and draw inspiration from the life of a good and faithful man who simply tried to live out the words found in Micah 6:6-8: "And what does the Lord require of you? To act justly, to love mercy, and to walk humbly with your God."

EULOGY

MR. GORDON "YOGI" YARBOROUGH

Thursday, January 5, 2006
Providence Place, High Point, NC

Delivered by:
Paul J. Lessard, President, High Point Community Foundation

It has been over a year and a half now since my friend Yogi took me out to lunch to have what he called "the best barbecue in the world" at one of his favorite places, Lexington Barbecue. We enjoyed a great lunch, he teased the waitresses, we discussed life, family, God and everything in between, and you know, he was right – it really was great barbecue! Our friend, Yogi, knew barbecue.

After lunch, Yogi took me for a drive around Lexington. He wanted to show me where he grew up, where he went to school, the route he took when he had delivered newspapers as a young boy, and the fields where he played baseball and football with his friends. For the first time, I really began to understand Yogi's origins; I could see how, in the face of many challenges, he had pulled himself up by his own bootstraps in his life journey. I learned how much he loved his family, his friends, his community, and most of all I could see how well Yogi had used the gifts and talents that God had given him. Seeing it all only made me love and respect my friend even more. At one point he pulled off to the side of the road, turned off the engine, and just sat there for a moment looking out over a beautiful pasture. He finally turned to me and asked if I was wondering why he was showing me all this. I shrugged as I told him how much I had enjoyed it. It was then that he told me that he was going to die and that he wanted me to give his eulogy.

You see Yogi had recently been diagnosed with ALS, but he looked good and strong that day; he was still walking with his cane. He was a man so vibrant and full of life, and I remember looking at my friend and realizing for the first time that one day he would be gone. I remember thinking to myself that a world without Yogi Yarborough just wouldn't be the same.

Of course, I told him, I would give his eulogy; I was honored to be asked, for Yogi had always been a mentor and a dear friend whom I admired and loved. Most of all, he was a man I wished I could be more like.

In the year that followed, Yogi and I began meeting every Friday for lunch initially to help me prepare for his eulogy. We talked about his life, his loves, and the principles and values that he had embraced throughout his journey. These were the attributes that made Yogi the man who loved others so well, who gave without thought of recognition, who cherished his family, who was committed to his friends and who absolutely trusted his God in the good times as well as in times of adversity.

Over the course of the year, it became increasingly clear to me that not only would I tell Yogi's story at his funeral, I would also write a book about the journey he and I were taking together that would preserve his memory for two very special children, Nathan and Maggie, Yogi's grandchildren. I realized as I walked arm and arm with my friend during that last year that it was important for these children he loved so deeply to know who their grandfather really was, what he stood for, what he cared about and how much he loved them.

So, for the next few moments, I'd like to tell Nathan and Maggie about a very special man whose amazing heart has brought us all together tonight to celebrate a life well lived and a race well run.

Nathan, your grandfather was a lover of people, which is a very special gift, for Yogi loved his friends boldly, passionately and so completely. Those of you who worked with Yogi know that he considered each of you family; those he and Martha went to church with know that you also were considered family. His friendship knew no boundaries of race, color, income or zip code.

He understood that "It is only with the heart that one can see rightly ... that what is essential is often invisible to the eye." Your grandfather often talked about a dear friend of his named Mrs. Powers, an old blind woman who was very poor, very alone and very sick. Yogi visited her several times a week. He prayed with her, talked with her and listened to her. He took care of her, and because she had no family, he became her family. He would often take your father and Uncle Scott to pray with her. He once told me that Mrs. Powers had taught him about the depth and the breadth of God's love.

Your grandfather used to say that Mrs. Powers had so little, yet she was the richest woman in the world. He said that she possessed a peace that did indeed "surpass all human understanding." She taught your granddad that the secret to a happy life was being able and willing to lie back into God's hands and simply trust him. When Mrs. Powers knew she was dying, she asked your granddad to sit at the funeral as her very own son, an honor which he considered one of the most cherished recognitions he ever received during his lifetime.

Your granddad loved your grandmother so much and you could tell by the way he looked at her; it was a look that told you that she was the most important person in the whole world. They were soul mates, partners, and most of all, they were friends.

You could see how much he loved your father and Uncle Scott by the way he rejoiced in their lives, celebrated their achievements, mourned their losses and simply enjoyed their company.

Preston, your father loved your passion and your competitive spirit. He was so proud of the father you have become.

Scott, your father always loved your sincere heart and your driving desire to be God's man in the work place. He truly enjoyed your mutual love of the business world.

Mindy, your father-in-law loved how you loved his son and for giving him two of his precious gifts when you brought Nathan and Maggie into this world.

Whether it was gardening with you, Martha, going to a soccer match with you, Preston, traveling to New York with you, Scott, to watch the World Series, or playing on the floor with you, Nathan and Maggie... to Yogi, his family was the personification of God's love and grace in his life. He liked to say that your "souls met" and I believe they always will.

Maggie, your granddad was one of the most compassionate men I have ever known. He ached for those who lived in poverty, who were poor in spirit, who were abandoned and forgotten. One of my favorite things about Yogi was how he loved people exactly where they were. I know he gave a lot of people a small glimpse of what God's unconditional love looked like. Being loved like this is a powerful thing and it brought out the very best in all of us; that was what your granddaddy did best.

One day when you are older, you will understand that your grandfather grew up very poor; he knew what it was like to go without. One day, he was with your Uncle Scott and they were working at the homeless shelter giving away gifts to the families in need. As they left, your granddad turned to your Uncle Scott and smiled a sad smile. With tears in his eyes, he said that he knew how good it felt to receive a gift given in love, for he had been a recipient of gifts just like that from his church when he was young.

I could spend hours telling you about all the things your grandfather contributed to and believed in, the organizations he served, the students he sent to college and the incredible good he did with the resources with which God blessed him. But I know he would much rather me tell you about how important the gift of compassion is. He would want me to encourage you both to be willing to step out of your "comfort zone" so you too can reach out and love those who have been forgotten and discarded. He would want you to always think beyond yourselves and give not just your money, but your time, your energy and your heart so that, like your granddad, you will continue to change the world one life at a time.

Another thing your granddad was always known for was his willingness to struggle and persevere in the face of great adversity. He understood very early in life that circumstances should never determine your attitude, and he demonstrated this over and over again in his journey through life.

You could see his willingness to fight the good fight in his rise from poverty, his quest to get an education, his successes and challenges in sports, his battle with cancer (a fight that nearly killed him before he was even married to your grandmother), his bout with depression and even with his final struggle with ALS. Your granddad never gave up; he always clung to the words in the book of Romans which our mutual friend Clebe McClary has so elegantly written about and embraced: "We rejoice in our suffering because we know that suffering produces perseverance; perseverance character; and character hope. Hope does not disappoint us because God has poured out His love into our hearts by the Holy Spirit, whom He has given us."

He knew his God would never let him down.

Your granddad believed in being committed to his friends. When Yogi Yarborough loved you, you knew it. He would love you beyond the point of vulnerability, for he was a man who was always willing to bare his soul to those he cared about. That is so rare in the world today.

Yogi believed in friendships that were deep, accountable and profound. And I know he would tell you, as he once told your father and your Uncle Scott; "You must have friends in your life you can tell anything to and know they will still love you and accept you."

In the last year of his life, I watched how those who loved your granddad gathered around him and cared for this man who had loved them so well over the years. I can still see the faces of his friends who told the "Yogi stories" at his testimonial dinner, and I can still hear the unrestrained laughter that Yogi shared with his dear friend, Raymond Payne, a remarkable man who has cared so well for him during these last months. Yogi really loved you, Raymond, and I do, too.

There are only a few men in my life that I openly and unabashedly say I love you to; your granddad was one of them. May you both enjoy the gift of friendship and may you one day experience the love that your granddad was showered with in his final months.

Finally, I pray that both of you will know and trust God as your granddad did; without hesitation, without fear, without demands and anger, but with a blind faith that I believe is your true inheritance.

In the book of Hebrews is a definition of faith that your grandfather and I always liked: "Faith is the assurance of things hoped for and the conviction of things not seen." This is how your granddad lived his life, and I wish this for both of you and everyone in this room.

In these last few months, I have watched your granddad lose so much, but at the same time I saw him grow richer in his faith, his love, his wisdom, his patience and, most of all, his courage. He achieved a nobility of spirit that only comes from walking through the fire hand-in-hand with his savior, Jesus Christ.

So, you see, Nathan and Maggie, your granddad was a real live hero to me and so many others in this room tonight. Because of the way he loved and invested in us, we are better people for being "Yogi's Friends."

Always remember your granddad's laugh; remember his hugs; remember his voice; remember how much he loved being with you; remember all the good things he has stood for in his life. Know that he is now resting in God's loving arms; that he is no longer in pain, and, most of all, know that his spirit, his sweet, kind spirit, will always be with you and with all of us.

Tonight, we commend your grandfather, our friend, Yogi Yarborough, into the hands of his savior, in the company of great men and great souls...

ABOUT THE AUTHOR

Paul J. Lessard is the Founding President of the High Point Community Foundation which was established in 1998. Under Paul's leadership, the Foundation's assets have grown from $5 million to over $65 million. In the past 17 years the Foundation has given $4 million in unrestricted grants and $38 million in Donor Advised Fund grants that have impacted locally, statewide, nationally and internationally.

Paul earned his Bachelor of Arts in English and History at High Point College where he attended on a soccer/academic scholarship in the mid-70s. He earned his Master of Fine Arts in Communications from the University of North Carolina at Greensboro in the early 80s. He was selected to pursue Post-graduate Studies in Nonprofit Management at Harvard University Business School in the summer of 2006.

Paul is the Founder and Director of the *Lighthouse Project*. Established in 1994 with a monetary stipend that accompanied the Carnegie Hero Medal. For the past 20 years the Project has partnered with the Guilford County School's Character Education Program to bring in over 50 nationally known role models to share their stories of success and significance. To date the Project has impacted over 650,000 students.

Paul was awarded the Carnegie Hero Medal, our nation's highest civilian recognition for heroism, for saving an elderly woman from drowning in a submerged car in 1994. He received the Congressional Commendation for Heroism in 1994. He was awarded Key to the City, High Point, NC and Resolution of Commendation for Heroism, 1993.

He was selected "Community Hero" Olympic Torch Bearer for the Atlanta Olympics, 1996. He was named Polar Heart Monitor "Heart to Believe Success Story" Award Winner, 1998.

He was awarded the High Point Chamber of Commerce "Business Advocate of the Year" Award, 2002. He received the inaugural "Dr. Kennedy Humanitarian of the Year" Award for advocating for children, 2004. He was awarded the High Point Community Foundation's Achievement Award for 10 years of Inspirational Service to the High Point Community, 2008.

Paul has been featured in the *Wall Street Journal, Good Housekeeping Magazine, USA/Today Newspaper, and US News and World Report*. He has also been seen on NBC's *Olympic Moments* and PAX TV's *It's a Miracle* and the Lifetime Network's *Beyond Chance*.

Paul writes a widely read newspaper column, *Giving 101* that examines the art and science of giving, he has authored three books; *The Mean Little Princess* (Children's book), *Visions of Philanthropy* (Treatise on Giving) and *A Measure of My Heart, Life Lessons from Yogi* (Memoir to be released in fall of 2015). He is currently working on a book about his friendship with Greg Commander, a man who served 20 years in federal prison where he came to Christ and has since become a leading advocate for keeping kids out of gangs. Greg, who dropped out of school in the 8th grade, graduated from college in May of 2015 at the age of 47.

Paul is married to Jayne Issacson Lessard who is a psychologist in private practice. They have two children: daughter, Taylor, a labor/delivery nurse who recently has been accepted into the PA Program at High Point University and a son, Jordie, who just graduated from Wheaton College where he competed on the Soccer and Crew Teams. Paul's goal in life is to be a Godly husband to Jayne and a loving father to his children.